PASTORAL
Prayers
to Share

Year A

Also by David Sparks

Prayers to Share, Year A
Prayers to Share, Year B
Prayers to Share, Year C

David Sparks

PASTORAL
PRAYERS
TO SHARE

Prayers of the People
for Each Sunday
of the Church Year

YEAR A

Revised Common
Lectionary Based

Editor: Ellen Turnbull
Cover and interior design: Verena Velten & Chaunda Daigneault
Cover image: iStockphoto © imagedepotpro
Proofreader: Dianne Greenslade

WoodLake is an imprint of Wood Lake Publishing, Inc. Wood Lake Publishing
acknowledges the financial support of the Government of Canada, through the Book
Publishing Industry Development Program (BPIDP) for its publishing activities. Wood
Lake Publishing also acknowledges the financial support of the Province of British
Columbia through the Book Publishing Tax Credit.

At Wood Lake Publishing, we practise what we publish, being guided by a concern for
fairness, justice, and equal opportunity in all of our relationships with employees and
customers. Wood Lake Publishing is committed to caring for the environment and
all creation. Wood Lake Publishing recycles, reuses, and encourages readers to do the
same. Resources are printed on 100% post-consumer recycled paper and more environ-
mentally friendly groundwood papers (newsprint), whenever possible. A percentage of
all profit is donated to charitable organizations.

Library and Archives Canada Cataloguing in Publication
Sparks, David, 1938-
Pastoral prayers to share, year A : prayers of the people for each Sunday of
the church year / David Sparks.

"Revised Common lectionary based".
Includes indexes.
Accompanied by a data CD.
ISBN 978-1-55145-585-3

1. Pastoral prayers. 2. Church year--Prayer-books and devotions--English.
I. Title.

BV250.S59 2010   264'.13   C2010-904837-7

Published by WoodLake
An imprint of Wood Lake Publishing Inc.
9590 Jim Bailey Road, Kelowna, BC, Canada, V4V 1R2
www.woodlakebooks.com
250.766.2778

Printing 10 9 8 7 6 5 4 3 2 1
Printed in Canada by
Transcontinental

CONTENTS

GRATITUDES

My thanks go to those many persons at Wood Lake Publishing who have been involved in this Pastoral Prayers project.

I would especially like to mention Mike Schwartzentruber for gently encouraging me to start this venture; and editor Ellen Turnbull, for her tireless, thoughtful, and empathetic presence in enabling the book to come to publication. She has made "the rough places smooth," and through her editorial efforts and initiatives this has become a far more faithful and useful book at the end than it was when we first began the creative journey.

Thanks also to Verena Velten for the dramatically inspiring cover design and Chaunda Daigneault for her skilled work on the layout of the book. It is good to look at and easy to use.

Thanks to my wife, Kathy, for her loving support and encouragement in the long days of this writing project.

It is the people of the congregations where I have led worship that have shaped and inspired these prayers. Their joys, their sorrows, their dreams and testing times, their challenges, and their responses to the Christian year are mirrored in my words and prayer phrases. It is a huge responsibility to offer prayer Sunday by Sunday, and it has been the support of so many wonderful "persons of the pew" and their willingness to explore different ways of offering pastoral prayer that have made this book possible. I am deeply grateful.

David Sparks

INTRODUCTION

I have been encouraged and heartened by the response of worship leaders to the three volumes of *Prayers to Share*. These books have found a home on many a worship leader's bookshelf in North America, but also as far afield as the United Kingdom, Australia, and India.

As I participated in prayer workshops after the release of the books, many people told me that they found the responsive format very useful; it allowed congregational members and worship leaders to have a common involvement in the prayer offering. I also heard one particular question asked time and time again: "So what about pastoral prayers? We need some help with them as well!"

This lectionary based book, and the books for years B and C that will follow, are a response to that often-voiced request.

My conversations with worship leaders identified that most leaders find the retyping of words into a computer file very tedious! Thus, the print volume of *Pastoral Prayers to Share* includes a data CD for easy copying or manipulation of the material for printing or projection.

The online version of this volume of prayers has the same capability as the data CD. The transfer of prayer data can be done easily and swiftly and the task of modifying the prayer can be accomplished as and when the worship leader chooses.

Some worship leaders are not sure about the freedom to reproduce the prayers either in their existing or modified form. Put simply, you may reproduce any prayer included in this book for use within your own congregation without seeking the authority of anyone. If you intend to include a portion of the book in another publication, *you will need to contact Wood Lake Publishing for permission.*

As this book is the first of a series of three, the author and the publisher would welcome feedback on what might be changed or incorporated into the subsequent volumes for lectionary years B and C. Please send your comments to:

Ellen Turnbull
Editor
Wood Lake Publishing Inc.
9590 Jim Bailey Road
Kelowna BC V4V 1R2
ellent@woodlake.com

The pastoral prayer is a common enterprise of faith. Worship leaders and people together have the responsibility of offering to God those situations, persons, and challenges that concern our hearts, our minds, and our essential spirit.

We faithfully offer our prayers Sunday by Sunday in a world where the inroads of our materialist society threaten to erode completely the ancient and treasured life of faith. But does it do any good to pray for the world and its needs? Does it do any good to pray for our own needs? Could we not be doing something more useful? Will the next generation be a praying generation?

The questions will continually come to us, but at the end of the day we can only look to the one all-loving God and say, "We cannot cease from praying."

David Sparks
Summerland, B.C.

ABOUT PASTORAL PRAYER

A basic question as we come to pray pastorally is, "What are we attempting to do when we pray for others?"

What we are *not* trying to do is persuade God to act in a particular way in the world, or fulfill the wishes of the members of the faith community who are praying, or get ourselves out of work. That is, we are not trying to persuade God to do what we ourselves could do with some energy and effort.

So what *are* we about as pastoral pray-ers?

We are about bringing ourselves individually and as a faith community into right relationship with God. We do this because it is a necessary first step in fulfilling God's intention for earth's inhabitants: the establishment of God's realm or kingdom. Jesus also made this intention the central theme of his teaching.

We are also about expressing our compassion for suffering humanity. This is a basic need and desire for those who follow Jesus Christ.

It is the most natural act in the whole world to express to God what is in our heart, and to do so in company with faith community friends who share the same beliefs. In the same way that we rush to tell a best friend or well-loved family member of our joys and our deepest concerns, so without a moment's thought do we bring them to God. Even persons with little or no formal religious belief pray fervently to God when the chips are down!

We are about being willing to be involved in the answers to our own prayers. In his book *The Use of Praying*, J. Neville Ward puts the concept very well. He writes that our prayers are "a piece of work involving costly self-surrender for God, for the work God wants done on other souls."

And so we are challenged every time we offer or hear prayer to ask the question of ourselves, "What can we do to enable the good outcome, the outcome that will bring God's realm closer?" This may seem a little far fetched, and in some cases action may indeed be impossible, but as one who offers prayer, it is a good question to keep in mind.

So...*there is a famine in Ethiopia.* It is on the TV news night after night. It comes up in the pastoral prayer. We know that Ethiopia is thousands of miles away in Africa and we cannot personally take food and water to those who are suffering, but we are able to financially support the International Red Cross, or Doctors without Borders, who are able to care for the victims.

So...*a phrase in the pastoral prayer catches our attention.* It speaks of the need to "help those who are reluctant to go to the doctor" for consultation. The phrase reminds us of a friend who is agonizing over a persistent back pain; as a result of hearing the prayer (or writing it) we call up the friend and are with her in her decision to seek medical advice.

So...*a phrase in the prayer speaks of the need to support leaders in our local faith community.* We hear a call within the prayer to offer a word of thanks to those who serve our church without fuss, and to consider leadership within the church ourselves.

So...*a phrase in the prayer reminds us of the fact that God never leaves us in times when we feel depressed.* We have a close family member who is "in the dark valley." It is a stimulus to make that visit that we have been promising to make for a week or so. Or it may be that we are personally feeling low and need to hear the reassurance that God is with us in our miserable moments.

One of our responsibilities as a worship leader is to provide education about the significance and meaning of the pastoral prayer. It does not have the prominence in the service of the sermon, or the popularity of congregational song or hymns, and is often seen as one last thing to do before the final hymn and blessing. I have heard of one worship leader who will, if the service is running a little late, leave the pastoral prayer out altogether! I am certain that there is a need to regularly explain the purpose of the pastoral prayer, and that members of the congregation will be grateful for the explanation and feel involved as the prayer is offered.

HOW TO USE THIS BOOK

A step by step guide

The Prayers in This Book

In most of the formats used in this book, the prayer is divided into four sections. This split into four divisions gives a clearly recognized structure to the pastoral prayer and enables the worship leader to easily make changes and substitutions to the prayer phrases for each week of the church year. Icons in the margin allow quick identification of the sections as follows:

World	Suffering	Church	Ourselves
Prayers for the world, including prayers for persons or groups of persons in the local town, city, or municipality, and the neighbourhood.	*Prayers for the suffering,* including prayers for those who have suffered loss, those who are sick, those who are caregivers, the bereaved, and those who support them.	*Prayers for the church/faith community,* the local church, wider church groupings, and faith communities supported by mission money throughout the world.	*Prayers for ourselves.* Acknowledging the fact that persons worshipping have specific needs and want these to be recognized in the worship.

Preparing to Offer Public Pastoral Prayer

If you are to offer prayer on a given Sunday, the time to begin to think about the prayer is the Monday morning of the week before!

During the week, as you go about your responsibilities and conversations, as you encounter friends and church and family members and reflect with them on their joys, sorrows, frustrations, and challenges, remember that there may be a place for their situations in your pastoral prayer. And as you reflect on your own feelings and circumstances (the crisis at work, the bullying of one of your children at school), remember that these too could find a place in the prayer you offer.

Then there is the news media. As you read the newspaper, as you check the news that appears on your computer or BlackBerry, or as it is reported on television, be alert for items that make an impact on you or on others. They could find a place in your pastoral prayer. It could be an earthquake or conflict in the Middle East, or a local item, such as an interview with the parents of a well-known young person who is missing. If the story has got people talking or arguing, or if the story has an emotional impact, then it could form a phrase of the pastoral prayer.

There are aspects of offering public prayer that you need to carefully guard. **The privacy laws of your area or country should be strictly followed.** It is usually not permissible to mention the names of those who are in local hospitals or care homes unless you have their express permission. And the same goes for family members, especially children; be sure that you ask them directly if you want to include them or their situation in your prayer. Do not assume that they will not find out if they are in church school at the time of the pastoral prayer. They will!

If you are the sort of person who is well organized, keep a notebook beside your desk or in your pocket. It is helpful to jot down pastoral prayer ideas and topics as they come to you.

Give the pastoral prayer a regular place in your personal prayer life. Pray by name for those who are on your mind or in your heart, and who you need to hold up before God. Also listen out for those promptings that come to you in significant times of holy silence.

In this book, the language used is inclusive of gender as it relates to persons and as it relates to God. I would encourage you, the worship leader, to avoid a preference for male imagery and male pronouns.

I would also encourage you to carefully monitor the words that you use in prayer. For me, the comment of those who wrote the preface to *The Good News Bible* is a good guide: "Every effort · has been made to use language that is natural, clear, simple, and unambiguous." Words such as *righteousness* and *redemption* are not understood, or are misinterpreted by most persons in the pew these days. A good rule of thumb is to use words that appear in your daily newspaper or that are used during the television news.

At the end of the day, remember the words of Thomas Merton: We do not want to be beginners [at prayer]. But let us be convinced of the fact that we will never be anything but beginners, all our life!

Different Formats

There are many ways to offer the pastoral prayer. Below is a description of the ways used in this book. In most of the formats, the scripture theme for the readings in lectionary year A is followed. Usually the theme will follow the gospel reading.

The format used most often in this book is the two leaders/congregational response format. ***The words of the first leader are printed in bold italic.*** The words of the second leader are printed in regular type. **The words of the congregational response are printed in bold.**

Format 1: Two leaders with congregational response

One: *We live in Advent hope, O God.*
We await the coming of Jesus to our world.

Two: Jesus comes when there is a permanent peace.
Jesus comes when the poor amongst us are supported, and the developmentally and physically challenged are free to enjoy a fulfilled life.
Jesus comes when those with resources give gifts to those stressed for lack of holiday money.
Jesus comes when the wisdom of children is listened to and heeded.
In an uneasy world,

One: *we will work faithfully*

All: **to free the spirit of Jesus, God's Anointed One.**

NOTES

The trigger phrase we will work faithfully *and congregational response* **to free the spirit of Jesus, God's Anointed One** *would be printed in the bulletin or projected.*

The prayer may be also be offered by a single worship leader – simply ignore the bold italics.

Format 2: One leader with congregational response
and
Format 3: A personal (feeling) reflection on the Christian scriptures
(How we wish we could have been on Jordan's bank!).

One: How we wish we could have been on Jordan's bank! On Jordan's bank was a crowd of people seeking radical change in their life's direction.

We pray for those who face medical conditions that are difficult to diagnose or treat.

We pray for those who are held back by guilt over past wrongs, and for those who need the help of another to reveal their hidden gifts and talents.

We pray for those in spiritual crisis, who seek renewal and inspiration in their shadowed times.

We pray for those who find life fragmented and overwhelming.

We pray for those who are sick, for whom each new day is a struggle.

We pray for those who have lost loved ones and find it hard to break out of the tomb of bereavement *(time of silent reflection).*

As we pray that forgiveness and empowerment will be the reality for ourselves and for our friends,

One: *how we wish,*
All: **we could have been on Jordan's bank!**

Format 4: Use the key words of scripture as a peg on which to hang the prayer.

Isaiah 35, selected verses indicated by *

One: *This is our hope, O God, that, "the ransomed of the Lord will return, and come to Zion with singing."* *

Two: This is our hope, O God, that revival will burst out in our faith communities,
and vibrant worship and selfless service will be marks of our local and mission projects.
This is our hope, O God, that faith communities will serve together in the local community.

One: *It seems a far off hope,*

All: **but with faithful effort, it will become joyful reality.**

One: *This is our hope, O God, that, "they shall obtain joy and gladness, and sorrow and sighing will flee away."* *

Two: This is our hope, O God, that the fears which hold us bound will be faced,
and the talents we keep hidden will be used.
This is our hope, O God, that the anxiety that we do not speak of will be expressed,
and worries about family members will be shared.

One: *It seems a far off hope,*

All: **but with faithful effort, it will become joyful reality.**

Format 5: Use people and objects to illustrate and emphasize.

White Gift Service Intergenerational Prayer
An Eyes-Open Prayer to be prayed slowly.

A young person holds up battered rag doll, while another holds up a new computer game in a shiny box.

One: We pray for boys and girls who have few gifts this Christmas.

All: **Help us, O God, to help them.**

The young person with the shiny toy gives it to the one with the rag doll.

An adult holds up a packet of pasta, while another holds up a fancy box of chocolates.

One: We pray for families for whom Christmas will just be
      another tough day.

All: Help us, O God, to share with them.

The person with the chocolates exchanges them for the pasta.

Format 6: Follow the theme of the scripture. This is the usual format for the prayers in this book.

Isaiah 7:10–16
Matthew 1:18–25

Jesus is born to Mary, Joseph has a dream.

One: *Jesus is born to Mary. Joseph dreams of a saviour.*
      The world will never be the same again!

Two: Families living below the poverty line receive
      government help, and challenged children get the
      support they need.
      Women and men labouring in sweatshops earn a fair
      wage in a safe and clean workplace.
      Those who speak another language are treated with
      respect, and those from different cultural backgrounds are
      given the opportunity to follow their trade or profession.
      A lack of money is no longer a barrier to higher
      education, nor influence the way to a secure job.

One: *Jesus was born the Saviour,*

All: and we will bring salvation in our own time.

One: *Jesus is born to Mary. Joseph dreams of a saviour.*
      The struggling will never be the same again!

Two: Families beset with conflict agree to mediation, and children
      at odds with their parents find ways to resolve differences.
      Hard-pressed health professionals face their challenges,
      and frustrated patients come to terms with a slow
      return to health.
      The dying feel God's peace, and the bereaved know the
      comfort of friends.
      We bring to mind those we know *(time of silent reflection).*

One: *Jesus was born the Saviour,*

All: and we will bring salvation in our own time.

Format 7: Base the prayer on a hymn.

For example, sing a verse of *In Suffering Love* (*Voices United* #614) before each section.

All: Sing verse one: *In suffering love the thread of life…*
One: ***In suffering love,***
Two: we pray for those who are caught up in the conflicts of our world in *(insert current event)*.
One: ***In suffering love,***
Two: we pray for those for whom the basic necessities of life cannot be taken for granted.
We think of those forced to live on the streets because there is no suitable housing.

All: Sing verse two: *There is a rock, a place secure…*
One: ***In suffering love,***
Two: we pray for those within the church who are going through hard times;
those in the wider church for whom the support of the mission fund is the difference between a fulfilling life or a meagre existence.

All: Sing verse three: *In love's deep womb…*
One: ***In suffering love,***
Two: we pray for those who are traumatized because of sexual or physical abuse, or because they were not allowed to speak their own language in residential schools.
We feel for the suffering; we will work and give to end suffering.
We pray for those who are sick, and those denied access to places because of physical limitations.
We pray for those for whom bereavement is a numbing reality, and for whom the time of bereavement seems an endless, hopeless time.

All: Sing verse four: *Now to our hearts…*
One: ***In suffering love,***
Two: we remember the hard places of our own lives,
the anguish we feel that we are unable to share with those close to us,

the worry which is ours for members of our family, or
for our friends,
the chance happenings in life which have put us at a
disadvantage,
which have diminished full and free living.

All: Sing verse five: *In suffering love...*
One: ***In suffering love,***
Two: we remember the suffering of Jesus,
his suffering for others, his own suffering and death on
the cross.
We remember how he overcame death and knows risen
freedom.
In that hopeful spirit, we offer our prayers for others
and acknowledge our responsibility for others.
In that hopeful spirit, we believe our own suffering will
be lovingly transformed.

Format 8: Use *part* of a hymn as the congregational response.

Prayer of Thanksgiving
The people's chorus is the first verse of *Now Thank We All Our God*
(*Voices United* #236).

One: ***Thanks beyond measure, O Most Gracious God,***
for those who join us around the table today and
tomorrow, and for those family members and
friends who cannot be with us
Two: because of the cost of travel,
because of ill health,
because of conflict,
because they live so far away.
Thank you, God, for family and friends.
All Sing: Now thank we all our God, with heart, and
hands and voices...

One: ***Thanks beyond measure Creator God, for your gifts***
that nourish and sustain.
Two: You have given us the bounty on our table.
May your gentle endurance be found with those who
till the soil, harvest the crops, and raise animals,

and may your spirit of justice enable us all to keep earth
and creation good for our children and grandchildren.
Thank you, God, for all your good gifts in creation.
All Sing: Now thank we all our God...

One: *Thanks beyond measure health-giving God, for*
vitality, strength, and appetite.
Two: May your compassion be strong for those who are sick
in mind and body,
and those who are moving towards life's end,
and those who mourn the loss of a loved one.
May your compassion come alive through us.
Thank you, God, for health and strength.
All Sing: Now thank we all our God...

One: *Thanks beyond measure, God of the church, for a faith*
community of praise and prayer, of song and learning:
Two: a community of mutual support,
a community concerned for those without food or work
or shelter,
a faith community here at *(name)* and in the wider
church community *(name)*,
and through the mission fund that brings healing and hope
in other parts of Canada and throughout the world.
Thank you God, for the church.
All Sing: Now thank we all our God...

One: *Thanks for your gifts to each one of us, Loving God:*
Two: for your creative, sustaining, and hopeful presence;
for courage and creativity in each new day;
for Jesus Christ who inspires and challenges us.
Thank you God, for being with us.
All Sing: Now thank we all our God...

Format 9: Use a fully responsive format.

One: God is alive!
We see God stressed with the military forces and civilians
in a warzone *(current area of conflict)*.
All: How much danger do they have to endure?
One: We see God despairing about the refugees in Darfur
Sudan.

All: **Will nobody give them the attention they deserve?**
One: We see God juggling home and work with the parents of
    young children.
All: **Are there enough hours in the day?**
    God is alive! We are on God's side.

God is alive!
We find God sitting frustrated in an overcrowded emergency
    department.
We find God struggling with an unforeseen diagnosis.
We find God on the ward with overworked medical staff.
We find God with a bereaved person coming to terms
    with a harsh new reality.
We think of those we know who are suffering *(time of silent*
    reflection).
God is alive! We are on God's side.

God is alive!
God is with us as we go about the work of this local faith
    community:
its worship, its committees, its service to others.
God is with us as we support the wider church group *(name this)*
God is with us as we encourage the downhearted or teach
    young persons new skills,
and bring justice to women through the mission fund.
God is alive! We are on God's side.

God is alive!
God is our friend and helps us to work out a fresh way ahead
    in challenging relationships.
God is our friend and holds us steady when the pressure
    is on at work or socially.
God is our friend and goes with us when we strive to bring
    our dreams to reality.
God is the one friend who places no demands or time
    constraints on friendship.
God is alive! We will be on God's side.

NOTE

*The fully responsive format will be the natural way to go when a
projected version of the liturgy is used.*

Format 10: Use silence for effect.

The Parable of the Sower – A Pastoral Prayer

One: Stony ground: the continuing distrust between faith groups in our nation and in the world; the hate bred by prejudice and ignorance.

All: **Stony ground: those affected by acts of terrorism in *(name)*** *(time of silent reflection)*.

One: Stony ground: illness that will not yield to treatment, delay in treating needy patients due to staff shortages. We think of those we know who are ill *(time of silent reflection)*.
These persons are on our minds.

All: **Stony ground: frustrating relationships, family differences for which there seem no resolution, no change.**

One: Stony ground: the barren, empty place of bereavement. We think of those we know who have lost loved ones *(time of silent reflection)*.
These persons are in our hearts.

All: **Stony ground: that feeling of being stuck in circumstances that cannot be changed.**

One: Stony ground: fears hidden deep within us that cannot be released.

All: **Stony ground: a faith life that is stale and unrewarding** *(time of reflection)*.
If we can identify the stony ground, we have taken the first step in bringing change.
Loving God, may renewed determination bring a harvest of new opportunity and new direction. May a willingness to express our fears bring a harvest of freedom. May an exploration into aspects of our faith bring a joyful and spiritual harvest.

Format 11: The prayer is read silently by the congregation.

The leader begins the prayer with a simple phrase, such as, "Death is defeated, Jesus lives." In *silence*, the congregation reads the subsequent phrases printed in the bulletin or projected. Then the leader says the trigger phrase, and the congregation responds.

> **One: *The tomb is empty. Jesus lives!*** (Or after Easter
> Sunday use, ***Death is defeated, Jesus lives.***)
> *Leave 45–60 seconds silence for reading and reflection.*
>
> read in silence {
> The world will be a better place!
> The peacemakers will find a way to end the fighting in
> *(current example)*.
> The reasons for the abuse and neglect of seniors living
> alone will be determined, and action taken.
> Hope will come to the homeless in our area through
> *(local initiatives)*.
> Struggling students will find a person who enlivens
> their studies.
> }
>
> **One: *Jesus lives,***
> **All: hope is alive!**

Format 12: Use physical action as part of the prayer.

> **Good Friday**
>
> **All: We come to the cross,** *(a nail is hammered into a
> wooden cross)*
> **we look up,** *(a nail is hammered in)*
> **we see the broken Christ,** *(a nail is hammered in)*
> One: and we pray for those broken in our world.
> We pray for refugees who have had to flee from their
> homes and communities.
> We pray for boys forced to fight, and girls forced into
> prostitution.
> We pray for those hated by their neighbours or bullied
> by their peers.
> We pray for the broken,
> **All: and God calls us to reflection and to action.**

Format 13: Dialogue with the congregation before one or more of the prayer sections.

An example of a prayer for which a pre-section dialogue would be useful is the one for Season of Pentecost Proper 21 (Matthew 21:23–32) where Jesus is questioned about the source of his authority.

Dialogue with the congregation about who positive authority figures are for them as employers, caregivers, church leaders, and personally. They might also include world and national leaders. If possible, when the prayer is offered, include some of the names mentioned.

One: *Who has the authority to bring change to those who are going through tough times?*

Two: We respect those employers who are sensitive to the family needs of their employees

and who are understanding when personal crises arise. We remember... *(Jeff, the HR manager at the ABC Mill, etc.).*

We value family members and friends who understand when a cherished one is going through a challenging time, and stick with them. We think of ... *(Jill's mom, Rae, etc.).*

We respond to medical professionals who take the time to explain the diagnosis carefully, and ask for questions... *(like Dr. Karikan at the Family Clinic, etc.).*

We value those who recognize the devastating effects of bereavement or loss, and offer support for the long haul. We have heard about *(Bill's friend Lee, etc.).*

We pray for those we know in our own family, in our church family *(time of silent reflection).*

One: *The authority of Jesus came from the Living God,*
All: **and God stands ready to empower us to bring change for good.**

Format 14: Dialogue and dramatization will bring the prayer alive and will ensure it is remembered.

Both formats will mean that the prayer lasts longer, but why not have a shorter sermon that week?

For example, use the phrase from the Season after Pentecost Proper 13 prayer, "The call for mission to the neighbourhood would meet with a ready response."

Christine: I would like to see us going out to tell people in *(town/city)* what we are doing here at St. Andrew's. Maybe two by two like the disciples did in the Bible.

Jim: Sounds too much like evangelism to me. I think we would get a lot of doors shut in our faces.

Christine: Well, the locals are not rushing through our doors as it is, and we have a good worship service and fine youth activities. Why not tell people around us about it?

Jim: Well...perhaps...I would need some training before I went out.

Christine: And we will make sure you get it!

Format 15: The extemporary prayer.

All the previous ways of offering pastoral prayers assume that the worship leader will follow a format that is set down in a printed form. It may be adjusted or used as a template, but the basic form will be followed.

The extemporary prayer is offered at the service by the worship leader without any printed guide. Sometimes the prayer is the result of much prayerful preparation (the same preparation detailed earlier), and sometimes the worship leader relies on the Holy Spirit to directly guide him/her in what he/she is to say at the pastoral prayer time of the service.

Faithfully offered extemporary pastoral prayers are wonderful. Those offered by a thoroughly prepared worship leader with confidence in his/her ability to pray freely are most effective, but the worship leader who has done little or no preparation and relies on "the Spirit" to get them out of trouble usually ends up with an ineffective and longwinded prayer.

The controversy between those who use written forms of prayers and those who use extemporaneous prayers has been going on for centuries. The 17th-century diarist Samuel Pepys records that he was in a "hot dispute" with the ship's chaplain about extemporary prayer on a voyage to Holland back in 1660.

The worship leader who has no experience in offering extemporary prayer would do well to try out the medium in a safe environment before using it in a worship service. Prayer offered at the end of a time of small group learning in the faith community might be a way of getting started.

A good rule of thumb is to use extemporaneous prayer in public worship only when you feel confident and comfortable enough to do so.

Format 16: Devise your own prayer.

Feel free to experiment and improvise with your own ways of offering prayer.

As worship leader, the prayer is yours and you may add, alter, or delete the suggested text as you wish. Perhaps there are one or more of the phrases that you feel need changing in light of current or world or community situations. Feel free to make the changes. Perhaps the responsive phrase at the end of the prayer does not work for you. Replace it with a responsive phrase that rings true. Perhaps one word sums up for you the essence of the whole gospel reading for that Sunday. Compose a prayer with that word in mind and trust the source of your inspiration and your own words.

As worship leader, you have your unique prayer voice, and the pastoral prayer is one of the places in the service to find and develop it. Don't be afraid to experiment with different forms of prayer or to use words or illustrations that feel right but that you haven't used before.

A good rule of thumb is to ask yourself if the members of the congregation will remember the prayer when they get home. And more importantly, will the prayer inspire them to get involved in the answer to one or more of the prayer issues?

Type of write out your prayer and read it out loud before you use it in public worship. The act of articulation prior to the service will save you from having to make changes as you deliver it. Ask a close friend or your partner to listen to the prayer and ask them:

- Does this make sense to you?
- What have I left out?

Respect their responses.
Go to it!

SEASON OF ADVENT
Advent 1

LECTIONARY READINGS
Isaiah 2:1–5
Psalm 122
Romans 13:11–14
Matthew 24:36–44

The beginning of the Advent season. We await the coming of Jesus with hope.

We live in Advent hope, O God.
We await the coming of Jesus to our world.
Jesus comes when there is a permanent peace.
Jesus comes when the poor amongst us are supported, and the developmentally and physically challenged are free to enjoy a fulfilled life.
Jesus comes when those with resources give gifts to those stressed for lack of holiday money.
Jesus comes when the wisdom of children is listened to and heeded.
In an uneasy world,
we will work faithfully
to free the spirit of Jesus, God's Anointed One.

We live in Advent hope, O God.
We await the coming of Jesus to the tested ones.
Jesus comes when those who struggle daily with pain receive help.
Jesus comes when the depressed and downhearted find a trusted friend.
Jesus comes when the caregivers are noticed and affirmed.
Jesus comes when those who have lost loved ones are given the time and the space to mourn their loss *(time of silent reflection).*
Among the troubled and distressed,
we will work faithfully
to free the spirit of Jesus, God's Anointed One.

We live in Advent hope, O God.
We await the coming of Jesus Christ to the church.
Jesus comes when our church acknowledges its good and
    proven traditions, yet is not afraid to move beyond them.
Jesus comes when our music throbs with life and we sing in
    harmony.
Jesus comes when our church seeks other denominations and
    faith groups as partners in healing, promoting justice, and
    communicating the faith.
Jesus comes when our church looks outward to the needs of
    local and international communities and responds to them
    in gift and deed.
As friends and members of the faith community,
we will work faithfully
to free the spirit of Jesus, God's Anointed One.

We live in Advent hope, O God.
Each of us awaits the coming of Jesus Christ.
Jesus comes when we give priority to prayer and reflection in
    our busy lives.
Jesus comes when we follow his word and his way as faithful
    disciples.
Jesus comes in the taking of bread and wine.
Jesus comes when we realize the strength of our faith partners
    to support us, and the glorious communion of the saints
    who have gone before us.
As we reflect on our own experience and situation,
we will work faithfully
to free the spirit of Jesus Christ, God's Anointed One.

Another Way

1. Sing a verse of an Advent hymn, such as *Hope Is a Star* (*Voices
   United* #7) before and after each section.

2. At the end of each section, pose a question and leave time for
   silent reflection.

(use first stanzas from world section above)
…Jesus comes when the wisdom of children is listened to and
    heeded.

How can we help those for whom the time before Christmas is
a time of anxiety?
(Time of silent reflection.)
In an uneasy world,
we will work faithfully
to free the spirit of Jesus Christ, God's Anointed One.

(use first stanzas from suffering section above)
...Jesus comes when those who have lost loved ones are given
the time and the space to mourn their loss.
How are we able to help those we know who are troubled and
distressed?
(Time of silent reflection.)
We will work faithfully
to free the spirit of Jesus Christ, God's Anointed One.

(use first stanzas from section above)
...Jesus comes when our church looks outward to the needs
of the local and international communities and responds to
them in gift and deed.
As friends and members of the faith community, what part are
we able to play to build up the church?
(Time of silent reflection.)
We will work faithfully
to free the spirit of Jesus Christ, God's Anointed One.

(use first stanzas from section above)
...Jesus comes when we realize the strength of our faith
partners to support us, and the glorious communion of the
saints who have gone before us.
(Time of silent reflection.)
Will our own words and actions bring hope at this time of year?
We will work faithfully
to free the spirit of Jesus Christ, God's Anointed One.

3. **A placard with "Jesus is coming" printed on it is held up. After
each section of the prayer, add or mime a sign of peace, of
compassion, mission for the church, and prayer.**

Advent 2

LECTIONARY READINGS
Isaiah 11:1–10
Psalm 72:1–7, 18–19
Romans 15:4–13
Matthew 3:1–12

> *John the Baptizer appears out of the desert, a confrontational, charismatic, prophetic figure.*

How we wish we could have been on Jordan's bank!
On Jordan's bank, men and women were given a vision of
  a new realm.
We pray for the prophets of today:
the prophets who speak out for clean water and unpolluted air,
the prophets who warn of the extinction of plant and animal
  species,
the prophets who expose the horrors of child labour wherever
  it is found,
the prophets who expose the commercial focus of this holy time.
And though we need to listen to our own prophets,
how we wish
we could have been on Jordan's bank!

How we wish we could have been on Jordan's bank!
On Jordan's bank was a crowd of people seeking radical
  change in their life's direction.
We pray for those who face medical conditions that are
  difficult to diagnose or treat.
We pray for those who are held back by guilt over past wrongs,
  and for those who need the help of another to reveal their
  hidden gifts and talents.
We pray for those in spiritual crisis, who seek renewal and
  inspiration in their shadowed times.
We pray for those who find life fragmented and overwhelming.
We pray for those who are sick, for whom each new day is a
  struggle.
We pray for those who have lost loved ones and find it hard
  to break out of the tomb of bereavement *(time of silent
  reflection)*.

As we pray that forgiveness and empowerment will be the
reality for ourselves and for our friends,
how we wish
we could have been on Jordan's bank!

How we wish we could have been on Jordan's bank!
On Jordan's bank was a crowd who glimpsed Jesus, God's
Holy One, who would transform their lives.
The ministry of Jesus began with John. We remember that we
stand in the faithful tradition of the Baptized One.
The ministry of Jesus began with John. We rejoice that we
stand in the compassionate tradition of the Baptized One.
The ministry of Jesus began with John. We rejoice that we stand in
the just and prophetic tradition of the Baptized One.
As we seek to play our part in the faith community, as we
remember the vocation of Christian ministry,
how we wish
we could have been on Jordan's bank!

How we wish we could have been on Jordan's bank!
The questions call us to respond.
Can we make the turnaround to which we are called?
Are we ready to listen to the voice of the prophets?
Have we the commitment to step forward confidently?
Can we recognize Christ in the needy crowd around us? *(Time
of silent reflection.)*
As we struggle with the questions,
how we wish
we could have been on Jordan's bank!

Another Way

1. **Sing a verse of one of the *John the Baptizer* hymns, such as
   On Jordan's Bank (*Voices United* #20) after each section.**

2. **Turn this into a fully responsive prayer.**

How we wish we could have been on Jordan's bank!
**On Jordan's bank was a crowd who glimpsed Jesus,
God's Holy One, who would transform their lives.**
The ministry of Jesus began with John. We remember that we
stand in the faithful tradition of the Baptized One.

**The ministry of Jesus began with John. We rejoice
that we stand in the compassionate tradition of the
Baptized One.**
The ministry of Jesus began with John. We rejoice that we
stand in the just and prophetic tradition of the Baptized
One.
**As we seek to play our part in the faith community, as
we remember the vocation of Christian ministry,
how we wish we could have been on Jordan's bank.**

Follow the same pattern for the other sections.

3. The worship leader dresses up as John the Baptizer and wears
   a rough coat, sandals, and a wild look.

Advent 3

LECTIONARY READINGS
Isaiah 35:1–10
Psalm 146: 5–10 or Luke 1:47–55
James 5:7–10
Matthew 11:2–11

The prophetic hopes joyfully fulfilled!

**This is our hope, O God, that "the wilderness and the dry
land will be glad, and the desert will rejoice and blossom."**
This is our hope, O God, that the forces that lead to global
warming will be countered,
and those who promote green energy solutions will be heeded.
This is our hope, O God, that those who speak out for war will be
overwhelmed by those who work persistently for peace.
This is our hope, O God, that political prisoners will be
noticed, and that lives currently wasted in jail will be given
a fulfilling future.
This is our hope, O God, that students who struggle will find
teachers who enable them to blossom.
This is our hope, O God, that artists, writers, and movie
makers will be given the opportunities they deserve.
**It seems a far off hope,
but with faithful effort, it will become joyful reality.**

**This is our hope, O God, that you will "strengthen the weak
hands, make firm the feeble knees, and say to those who
are of feeble heart, 'Be strong, do not fear!'"**
This is our hope, O God, that those who are shy or lonely
will find a friend who takes the time to understand and
appreciate them.
This is our hope, O God, that children all over the world will
get the priority medical treatment they need.
This is our hope, O God, that those anxious about the results
of medical tests or a new course of treatment will know
reassurance.
This is our hope, O God, that those who have suffered the loss
of a cherished dream or a loved one will have a companion
to support them.

We remember those we know who are downhearted and sick,
and those who have lost loved ones *(time of silent reflection)*.
It seems a far off hope,
but with faithful effort, it will become joyful reality.

*This is our hope, O God, that "the ransomed of the Lord
will return and come to Zion with singing."*
This is our hope, O God, that revival will burst out in song
and fellowship in our faith communities.
This is our hope, O God, that vibrant worship and selfless
service will be the marks of our local and mission projects.
This is our hope, O God, that faith communities will serve
together to help the powerless and voiceless.
It seems a far off hope,
but with faithful effort, it will become joyful reality.

*This is our hope, O God, that "they shall obtain joy and
gladness, and sorrow and sighing will flee away."*
This is our hope, O God, that our disappointments will be faced.
This is our hope, O God, that the fears which hold us bound
will be let go.
This is our hope, O God, that the anxiety we do not speak of
will be expressed.
This is our hope, O God, that our worries about family
members will be shared.
It seems a far off hope,
but with faithful effort, it will become joyful reality.

Another Way

1. **Have the scripture quotes read by a person other than the
   worship leader/s.**

2. **Base the prayer on Matthew 11:2–11.**

God's messenger John prepares the way.
We will support those who work for peace in the Middle East
and *(current trouble spot)* where violence has been a way of
life for generations.
We will be ready to give generously to *(named Christmas
charity groups)* who in the past have found it difficult to
meet the needs of struggling persons.

We will be aware of the needs of those in far off places who wish they could be home at Christmastime.

We will go out of our way to offer our attention and peace to persons imprisoned by circumstance and forgotten in the hectic rush.

John prepares the way.
We will follow it carefully.

God's messenger John prepares the way.

We prepare for Christmas as we remember family members who are downhearted and stay beside them.

We prepare for Christmas as we share the joy of children and grandchildren, and catch the excitement of friendly boys and girls.

We prepare for Christmas as we support the caregivers and visit those in long stay homes.

We prepare for Christmas as we make contact with those who are sick and in hospital.

We prepare for Christmas as we offer comfort to those for whom Christmas brings back the feelings of personal loss.

We remember those for whom we pray *(names) (time of silent reflection)*.

John prepares the way.
We will follow it carefully.

God's messenger John prepares the way.

And our church responds with its own preparation.

We will put heart and soul into the songs and hymns and carols of Advent and Christmas.

We will find those who are not able to come to our services and special events and bring Word, song, and friendship to them.

We will prepare for the familiar nativity scene but be ready to move beyond it to the meaning of Jesus' birth for today.

We will be ready to give generously to our mission funds as well as to the local church.

John prepares the way.
We will follow it carefully.

God's messenger John prepares the way.

And we realize that each one of us has preparations to make apart from gifts, travel, and hospitality.

We will allow space in the busy-ness of Advent to think about the coming of Jesus, God's anointed one.

We will look at the way John called people to acts of
repentance and forgive those we can't seem to forgive at any
other time.

As we prepare to receive and give gifts, we will ponder on the
gifts we have to offer in the service of our fellow women
and men.

**In looking at John's preparation for the coming of Jesus,
we find that we too are called to prepare.**

Advent 4

LECTIONARY READINGS
Isaiah 7:10–16
Psalm 80:1–7, 17–19
Romans 1:1–7
Matthew 1:18–25

The birth of Jesus to Joseph and Mary.

Jesus is born to Mary. Joseph dreams of a saviour.
The world will never be the same again!

Families living below the poverty line receive government
   help, and challenged children get the support they need.
Women and men labouring in sweatshops earn a fair wage in
   a safe and clean workplace.
Those who speak another language are treated with respect,
   and those from different cultural backgrounds are given the
   opportunity to follow their trade or profession.
A lack of money is no longer a barrier to higher education,
   nor influence the way to a secure job.

Jesus was born the Saviour,
and we will bring salvation in our time.

Jesus is born to Mary. Joseph dreams of a saviour.
The struggling will never be the same again!

Families beset with conflict agree to mediation, and children at
   odds with their parents find ways to resolve differences.
Hard-pressed health professionals face their challenges, and
   frustrated patients come to terms with a slow return to health.
The dying feel God's peace, and the bereaved know the
   comfort of friends.
We bring to mind those we know *(time of silent reflection)*.

Jesus was born the Saviour,
and we will bring salvation in our time.

Jesus is born to Mary. Joseph dreams of a saviour.
The faith community will be transformed!

Unassuming do-ers and caregivers are recognized and thanked.
Mission horizons are extended and far off communities enlivened.
Local neighbourhoods find a focus in the church, and hidden
   needs of the faith community are identified and met.

The talents of members are recognized and used in worship
and in faith community service.
Jesus was born the Saviour,
and we will bring salvation in our time.

 Jesus is born to Mary. Joseph dreams of a Saviour.
Each one of us will be inspired!
We have the courage to name and live our dreams.
We renew our friendships and listen to the deepest feelings of
our friends.
We find a cause and stay with it all the way.
We rejoice in our faith and serve carefully as disciples of Jesus
Christ.
Jesus was born the Saviour,
and we will bring salvation in our time.

Another Way

1. A hopeful Advent song, such as *I Am Walking a Path of Hope*
(*More Voices* #221) or the refrain to *Hope Is a Star* (*Voices
United* #7) may be sung after each section.

2. We can think of the situation of Mary and Joseph and use it as
a preface to the sections.

 Mary and Joseph were vulnerable people in a hostile situation.
For them, we would want a change for the better. We want
a change in our world as well.
We want families living below the poverty line to receive
government help, and challenged children to get the support
they need.
We want women and men labouring in sweatshops to earn a fair
wage, and working conditions to be made safe and clean.
We want those who cannot speak English or French to have
the chance to attend classes and immigrants to have their
qualifications recognized.
We want a situation where lack of money is no longer a
barrier to higher education,
nor influence the way to a secure job.
Jesus struggled to bring change in his lifetime.
We will bring change in our time.

Mary and Joseph were vulnerable people in a hostile situation. For them, we would want a change for the better. We want change to happen among the suffering today.

We see families beset with conflict agreeing to mediation, and children at odds with their parents finding a way to resolve differences.

We see hard pressed health professionals facing their challenges and frustrated patients coming to terms with a slow return to health.

We see the dying feel God's peace, and the bereaved know the comfort of friends.

We bring to mind those we know *(time of silent reflection).*

**Jesus struggled to bring change in his lifetime.
We will bring change in our time.**

Mary and Joseph were vulnerable people in a hostile situation. For them, we would want a change for the better. We want change in our church today.

We would like the unassuming do-ers and caregivers to be recognized and thanked.

We would like mission horizons extended, and local neighbour-hoods to understand that the church wants to help them.

We would like the unspoken and unmet needs of the faith community identified and met.

We would like the talents of members recognized and used in worship and in service.

**Jesus struggled to bring change in his lifetime.
We will bring change in our time.**

Mary and Joseph were vulnerable people in a hostile situation. For them, we would want a change for the better. We want change to happen with us this Christmastime.

We have dreams and ambitions and we want the courage to name and live our dreams.

We have friendships that are uncertain and drifting and we want to renew them.

We want the ability to listen to the deepest feelings of our friends.

We have talked about helping the needy and we want to find a cause and stay with it all the way.

We rejoice in our faith and want to serve carefully as disciples of Jesus Christ and we find it difficult to pay the price.

We are aware that Jesus faced the challenge to change in his time, and met it. We want nothing less.

SEASON OF CHRISTMAS
Christmas Eve/Day
Christmas, Proper 1 (Years A, B, C)

LECTIONARY READINGS
Isaiah 9:2–7
Psalm 96
Titus 2:11–14
Luke 2:1–14 (15–20)

The birth of Jesus far from the security of home.

Love will win through.
Refugees will get the treatment they deserve, the protection
and resettlement they need.
The unemployed will find the necessary support and retraining.
Those out in the cold in this chilling winter weather will find
shelter.
The lonely and friendless will know someone who appreciates
and cares for them.
***Love will win through, and God's love lies vulnerable and
waiting in a cold and drafty stable.***
Jesus will pattern that love for us.

Love will win through.
Gifts will be freely given by those who have plenty, and those
gifts will be joyfully received by those struggling at Christmas.
Those who maintain essential services over Christmastime
will be remembered by their families.
The sick will find celebration in hospital or at home with
family and friends around them.
The bereaved will be comforted and sustained and those who
have suffered deep loss will be ready for the new situation
that faces them.
***Love will win through, and God's love lies vulnerable and
waiting in a cold and drafty stable.***
Jesus will pattern that love for us.

Love will win through.
Church members will feel friendship and the power of
conversation bringing them closer together.
Those who seldom come to worship will be welcomed and
appreciated in the faith community.
God's love will encourage each churchgoer to support the
hungry and despairing in the world through the mission fund.
Members will be ready, willing, and able to serve the needy in
the local community (through food bank, women's shelter).
Love will win through, and God's love lies vulnerable and
waiting in a cold and drafty stable.
Jesus will pattern that love for us.

Love will win through.
And we will experience the love of close family and friends
building us up, showing us how much more we are able to
achieve.
Love will tune us in to the spiritual values that are at the
heart of the Christmas celebrations and encourage us to
strengthen our spiritual life.
And love will hold us close and bring home the treasure we
have in those who are nearest and dearest to us.
Love will win through, and God's love lies vulnerable and
waiting in a cold and drafty stable.
Jesus will pattern that love for us.

Another Way

1. **After each section, have a member of the congregation give a
   testimony of "love winning through."**

2. **Sing a verse of *Love Us into Fullness* (*More Voices* #81) before
   the prayer begins and after each section.**

3. **Turn the prayer into a questioning prayer with silence after
   one or two phrases.**

Will love win through?
Will those who maintain essential services know the
support of family and friends?

Will the sick ones will find the strength to endure the
  Christmas holiday?
Will they find celebration in a hospital ward, or at home, with
  family and friends around them?
(Time of silent reflection.)
Will the bereaved find those who will comfort and sustain
  them?
Will those who have suffered deep loss, those who have
  recently separated, those whose cherished pet has died, be
  ready for the new situation that faces them?
(Time of silent reflection.)
**Love will win through, and God's love lies vulnerable and
  waiting in a cold and drafty stable.**
Jesus will pattern that love for us.

Will love will win through?
Will church members and friends feel the love of friendship
  bringing us closer together?
And will the love of God encourage us to support the hungry
  and despairing through our mission fund?
(Time of silent reflection.)
Will the love of God empower us to serve the needy in the
  local community *(through food bank, women's shelter)*?
(Time of silent reflection.)
**Love will win through, and God's love lies vulnerable and
  waiting in a cold and drafty stable.**
Jesus will pattern that love for us.

Follow the same pattern for the other sections.

Christmas Day/Eve
Proper 2 (A, B, C)

LECTIONARY READINGS

Isaiah 62:6–12
Psalm 97
Titus 3:4–7
Luke 2:(1–7) 8–20

The shepherds praise God for the very best of good news.

Out of the cold, to the shelter of the wonder-full stable came the shepherds.

On this holy night, we thank you, O God, for those who strive for peace in a troubled world, and we pray for those who feel afraid.

On this holy night, we thank you, O God, for families and loved ones reunited at Christmastime, and we pray for those who we wish were with us.

On this holy night, we thank you, O God, for the comfort of a good home, and we pray for those who lack warm and safe shelter.

On this holy night, we thank you, O God, that work is over for a while, and we pray for those who by their labours enable the lights to shine out, the streets to be safe, and the planes to fly.

We will return to our small corner of the world as determined as the shepherds who experienced first-hand the good news
to be the good news of Jesus Christ to those around us.

Out of the cold, to the shelter of the wonder-full stable came the shepherds.

On this night of light, we thank you for those who bring comfort and healing to the sick and depressed, and we pray for those who cannot feel the joy of the season because of pain, anxiety, or worry about a loved one.

On this night of Mary's joy, we thank you for those who have experienced the safe arrival of a baby, and we pray for those expecting a child, who wait with gentle excitement and quiet concern.

On this night of light, we thank you for those who have come
through the darkness of grief, and we pray for those who
mourn the loss of a well-loved family member or friend.
Our prayers embrace those we think of tonight *(time of silent
reflection)*.
**We will return to our small corner of the world as
determined as the shepherds who experienced first-hand
the good news**
to be the good news of Jesus Christ to those around us.

 *Out of the cold, to the shelter of the wonder-full stable
came the shepherds.*
On this peaceful night, we thank you for the churches *(faith
communities)* of which we are a part, and we pray for those
who are searching for spiritual inspiration and a faith family.
On this peaceful night, we thank you for the gifts and abilities
which are ours to use,
and we pray for those who are unable or afraid to try new
skills or venture into the unknown.
On this peaceful night, we thank you that the awe, the hope,
and the joy of Christmas is a part of our experience, and we
pray that your love, O God, will have a central place with
our family and friends.
**We will return to our small corner of the world as
determined as the shepherds who experienced first-hand
the good news**
to be the good news of Jesus Christ to those around us.

Another Way

1. The prayer might be offered in three parts, one after each
   scripture reading. A candle may be lit after each section; these
   could be the candles of the Advent wreath.

2. Prayer of Rejoicing

 *The angels rejoiced, the shepherds rejoiced, and a new
mother and father rejoiced.*
Jesus was born.
We rejoice when the calm of Christmas peace descends on our
world.

We rejoice when the leaders of our world come to agreement.
We rejoice when family members and friends are reunited this
holiday season.
We rejoice when babies are born to parents who love them
and care for them.
We rejoice when orphaned and rejected children find loving
homes.
Glory to God in highest heaven,
and on earth peace.

*The angels rejoiced, the shepherds rejoiced, and a new
mother and father rejoiced.*
Jesus was born.
Among the suffering there is hope of healing.
Among the despised and downtrodden there is hope of
recognition.
Among the insecure and anxious there is hope of calm.
Among those who have suffered loss there is hope of a new
day *(time of silent reflection).*
Glory to God in highest heaven,
and on earth peace.

*The angels rejoiced, the shepherds rejoiced, and a new
mother and father rejoiced.*
Jesus was born.
We rejoice to hear God calling us and to work out that calling
in faith community.
We bring and share joy within our church family.
We are sensitive to the children of our church, and listen to
them.
We celebrate the families of our faith community and nurture
them.
We cherish the worldwide family of faith and support
vulnerable children.
Glory to God in highest heaven,
and on earth peace.

*The angels rejoiced, the shepherds rejoiced, and a new
mother and father rejoiced.*
Jesus was born.
We enter the stable and wonder at God's chosen child; we
reflect that within a family at risk, a family far from home,
God's love is found.

We realize that this is a birth that will encourage us to live
in harmony with persons of different race and economic
circumstance than ours.
We are sure that this child will strengthen us to work for
justice wherever we go.
Mary turns and smiles at us as we approach the crib.
Glory to God in highest heaven,
and on earth peace.

---

3. **Sing the first verse of *Angels from the Realms of Glory* (*Voices United* #36) after each section.**

Christmas Day
Proper 3 (A, B, C)

LECTIONARY READINGS

Isaiah 52:7–10
Psalm 98
Hebrews 1:1–4 (5–12)
John 1:1–14

The gospel writer John makes clear that Jesus is the light that shines in the darkness.

Jesus, the life that brings light to the world, is born. Glory to God!

In this light, peace between nations becomes possible, peace between *(insert own words)*.

In this light, reconciliation and reunion take place.

In this light, we remember and thank those who work while others have a holiday.

In this light, the infectious enthusiasm of the young is welcome and the wisdom of the old appreciated.

We will be among the bringers of the light.

**The light shines in the darkness,
and the darkness will not overcome the light.**

Jesus, the life that brings light to the troubled, is born. Glory to God!

To those who are in hospital or cannot travel, we bring the light of friendship to enliven them.

To those for whom depression and despair deaden the Christmas spirit, we bring the light of companionship to encourage them.

To those who feel the loss of a loved one acutely, we bring the light of comfort to give hope.

To those who feel at a loss spiritually, we bring the light of "the Word made flesh" to inspire them.

We remember those who need the light of Christ today
(insert own words and/or time of silent reflection).

We will be among the bringers of the light.

**The light shines in the darkness,
and the darkness will not overcome the light.**

Jesus, the life that brings light to the church, is born.
Glory to God!

In the church, song and carols have lightened our Christmas
time.

In the church, familiar scriptures and books like *A Christmas
Carol* and *How the Grinch Stole Christmas* have delighted us
once again.

In the church, the light of Christ shone out from the Advent
wreath for four weeks. The light reminded us of the reasons we
give gifts to our loved ones and to those with crying needs.

Through the work of the wider church, the light of Christ has
brought hope and a second chance to persons all over the
world.

We will be counted among the bringers of the light.
The light shines in the darkness,
and the darkness will not overcome the light.

Jesus, the life that brings light to each one of us, is born.
Glory to God!

We need the Christ-light to bring much needed peace after the
Christmas rush.

We need the Christ-light to bring joy and friendship to our
family gatherings.

We need the Christ-light to go with us to the despairing and
challenged in our local community.

We need the Christ-light to bring adventure to our New Year
looking forward.

We need the Christ-light to bring the spirit of questioning and
healthy doubting to our faith journey.

The Christ-light brings new life to us.
The light shines in the darkness,
and the darkness will not overcome the light.

Another Way

1. After each section is prayed, a candle is lit. These candles could
   also be the candles of the Advent wreath. At the end of the
   prayer all four candles are extinguished and a larger one lit.

2. Turn this into an "eyes open" prayer and engage the congregation in dialogue.

Jesus, the life that brings light to the world, is born. Glory to God!

In this light, peace between nations becomes possible – peace between *(insert own words)*.

Can you think of a country where you would wish for peace today?

In this light reconciliation and reunion take place.

Can you think of a situation where reconciliation is needed in our town/city/world?

In this light we remember and thank those who work while others have a holiday.

Do you know anyone who is working while we are worshipping?

In this light the infectious enthusiasm of the young is welcome, and the wisdom of the old appreciated.

Can you tell me of any youngsters who are full of joy and laughter, full of beans, today? We know why!

They bring light to us and we will be among the bringers of the light.

The light shines in the darkness,
and the darkness will not overcome the light.

Jesus, the life that brings light to the troubled, is born. Glory to God!

To those who are in hospital or cannot travel, we bring the light of friendship to enliven them.

To those for whom depression and despair deaden the Christmas spirit, we bring the light of companionship to encourage them.

Do you have friends or family members who are sick or in hospital today? Don't mention their names, but if you wish, let us know their situation.

To those who feel the loss of a loved one acutely, we bring the light of comfort to give them hope.

Do you have friends or family members who are mourning a loved one today? Don't mention their names, but if you wish, let us know their situation.

To those who feel spiritually at a loss, we bring the light of "the Word made flesh" to inspire them.

In silence we remember those whose faith seems without foundation today. We think of our own faith challenges (time of silent reflection).

We will be among the bringers of the light.
The light shines in the darkness,
and the darkness will not overcome the light.

Jesus, the life that brings light to each one of us, is born.
Glory to God!
We need the Christ-light to bring peace after the Christmas
rush. *(Candle is lit.)*
We need the Christ-light to bring joy and friendship to our
family gatherings. *(Candle is lit.)*
We need the Christ-light to bring adventure to our New Year
looking forward. *(Candle is lit.)*
We need the Christ-light to bring the spirit of questioning into
our faith journey. *(Candle is lit.)*
The Christ-light brings new life to us.
The light shines in the darkness,
and the darkness will not overcome the light.

---

3. Have 22 small candles on the Communion table and designate
   congregational members to come up and light one after each
   sentence of the prayer. Give them a copy of the prayer so they
   know when to light the candle.

1st Sunday after Christmas

LECTIONARY READINGS

Isaiah 63:7–9
Psalm 148
Hebrews 2:10–18
Matthew 2:13–23

*Joseph and Mary and Jesus travel widely and in fear,
to escape the anger of Herod.*

A map of the world is held up.

The journey to freedom in our world is not an easy one.
Oscar Romero, Nelson Mandela, and Mahatma Gandhi would
each attest to that.
The journey is one where the intentions of leaders and policy
makers need to be tested.
The journey is one where the oppressed will be challenged to
work together.
The journey is one where the downhearted need caring
companions.
The journey is one where authors, artists, and actors may
encounter political interference and prejudice.
The journey is one with no certain and satisfactory end.
We are called to stand beside the freedom seekers.
You call us to freedom, O God.
Give us courage for the journey.

A picture of a hospital is held up.

**The journey to freedom for the suffering is not an easy
one.**
There are friends and family members whose illnesses are
hard to diagnose.
There are those whose treatment seems unending, who see no
end to a pain-filled journey.
There are those who seek to bring healing, insight, and relief,
yet encounter the roadblocks of professional opposition and
government cutbacks.
There are physically challenged persons who wonder if their
requests for access to restaurants and washrooms will ever
be heard.

There are persons who have suffered the death of a loved one.
Are we are able to ease the pain of their journeys? *(Time of
silent reflection.)*
You call us to freedom, O God.
Give us courage for the journey.

A road map is held up.

The journey to freedom in the church is not an easy one.
We are aware that ancient creeds and worship patterns are not
easily changed.
We are aware that old tunes and hymn words have a
permanence about them.
We are aware that buildings may be difficult to leave behind,
and that the aura of a building is hard to dispel.
We are aware that contemporary theological ideas may be
hard to accept, that new ways of looking at scripture may be
disturbing.
We are aware that working with other denominations and
faith groups may be viewed with suspicion.
We will make clear new forms and ways.
You call us to freedom, O God.
Give us courage for the journey.

A local street map is held up.

Our personal journey to freedom is not an easy one.
The pattern of living forged in the family circle holds us back.
Putting off making decisions holds us back.
The fear of what others may think and say about us holds us
back.
The reluctance to take risks and go on adventures holds us back.
A lack of friends to go with us holds us back.
We find it difficult to follow the example of Jesus, who paid
for freedom with his life, although it brought freedom to so
many.
We are pilgrims on the Christian way.
You call us to freedom, O God.
Give us courage for the journey.

Another Way

1. Have members of the congregation hold up the maps/ pictures.

2. Before and after the prayer, sing verse two of *Bless Now, O God, the Journey* (*Voices United* #633).

3. Intersperse each phrase with the words *Give them freedom!* shouted out by the congregation. The leader will speak out with zest!

 The journey to freedom in our world is not an easy one.
Oscar Romero, Nelson Mandela, and Mahatma Gandhi would each attest to that.
The journey is one where the intentions of leaders and policy makers need to be tested.
Give them freedom!
The journey is one where the oppressed find strength when they work together.
Give them freedom!
The journey is one where the downhearted need caring companions.
Give them freedom!
The journey is one where authors, poets, and painters may encounter political interference and prejudice.
Give them freedom!
The journey is one with no certain and satisfactory end for the challenged ones.
Give them freedom!
We are able to ease the pain of the journey.
You call us to be freedom bringers, O God.
Give us courage for the journey.
Give us freedom!

 The journey for the suffering is not an easy one
For those whose illness is hard to diagnose
Give them freedom!
For those whose treatment is unending
Give them freedom! *(etc.)*

The journey for the church is not an easy one
For those who struggle to change worship patterns and
   introduce new creeds
Give them freedom!
For those who want to introduce new songs and music
Give them freedom! *(etc.)*

The journey for each of us is not an easy one
As we understand the influence of family on our attitudes
Give us freedom!
As we break away from the opinions of others
Give us freedom! *(etc.)*

You call us to experience freedom, O God.
Give us courage for the journey.
Give us freedom!

White Gift Service Intergenerational Prayer
An Eyes-Open Prayer (to be prayed slowly)

*A young person holds up battered rag doll, while another holds up a
new computer game in a shiny box.*
> We pray for boys and girls who will have few gifts this
> Christmas.
> **Help us, O God, to help them.**

The young person with the shiny toy gives it to the one with the rag doll.

*An adult holds up a packet of pasta, while another holds up a fancy box
of chocolates.*
> We pray for families for whom Christmas will just be another
> tough day.
> **Help us, O God, to share with them.**

The person with the chocolates exchanges them for the pasta.

Two young people stand with fists raised, scowling at each other.
> We pray for nations where there is war today *(insert names)*.
> **Help us, O God, to speak and work for peace.**

The two young persons smile and link arms.

*A child in smart clothes smiles smugly to the congregation; another,
dressed in a dirty/torn outfit, looks downcast.*
> We pray for those who, like Mary and Joseph, are far from
> home.
> We pray for refugees, and for those who are running for their
> lives.
> **Help us, O God, to support them.**

*The person with the smart clothes takes off her jacket and gives it to the
one with the torn outfit.*

*A child is being given some cough syrup by an adult; another is taking
the temperature and wiping the brow of a sick parent.*
> We pray for those who are sick at home or in hospital today.
> Remember those you know who are suffering *(time of silent
> reflection)*.
> We pray for friends and family.
> **Help us, O God, to encourage and help them.**

A single person sits in a chair.
> We pray for those who have lost a loved one.
> Do any of you in the congregation know the names of
> someone who has lost anyone? *(Time of silent reflection.)*
> We pray for family, friends, and church friends.
> **Help us, O God, to stay beside them.**

A child goes across and stands beside the person in the chair.

A child and an adult stand together as if looking out of the window.
> We pray for those family members and friends who are far
> from home.
> **Help us, O God, to keep in contact with them.**
> We pray for those in our faith community (church) who are
> feeling sad, or experiencing hard times.
> **Help us, O God, to be their friends.**

> We pray for ourselves. We remember the events we have to
> celebrate as well as the challenges before us in the coming
> week.
> **Help us, O God, to know that in the ups and downs of
> life, you are with us.**

SEASON OF EPIPHANY
Epiphany of the Lord

LECTIONARY READINGS
Isaiah 60:1–6
Psalm 72:1–7, 10–14
Ephesians 3:1–12
Matthew 2:1–12

*The wise men from the East search for and find
the child born to be king.*

*In the New Year we are searching for a world where justice
is the reality:*
A world where political leaders see beyond narrow national
interest;
a world where terrorists are denied a homeland;
a world where peaceful protest does not meet with violent
response;
a country where no child goes to school hungry;
a neighbourhood where each elderly person is respected;
a town/city where food banks and sheltered housing are
available and no one is left outside hungry in the cold.
Just and Holy God,
the star sign is our call to get involved.

In the New Year we are searching for the relief of suffering:
Time out for those whose routine is relentless;
a calm place for those in emotional turmoil;
patient friendships for those who are in pain;
staying power for medical and support staff in homes and
hospitals;
hopeful words for those who are depressed or fearful;
comfort for those who have suffered loss.
We pray for those within our families or our church family
who sick or bereaved *(time of silent reflection)*.
Just and Holy God,
the star sign is our call to get involved.

In the New Year we are searching for new life in our faith community:
To feel free to question and doubt on our faith journey;
to respond to the call to discipleship in fresh ways;
to review old traditions and to explore new paths;
to be alert to unforeseen avenues of Christian service and
    go there;
to value anew the gifts of our brothers and sisters in Christ.
Just and Holy God,
the star sign is our call to get involved.

In the New Year we are searching for a fresh appreciation of our own talents and abilities:
An eagerness to put behind us those failures that have
    compromised our self-esteem;
a readiness to face those areas of life that trouble us;
a willingness to try new leisure and work activities and live
    with challenges that arise;
a determination to search out new friends or friendship groups
    and face feelings of vulnerability *(time of silent reflection)*.
*In every effort we make to use our talents and abilities to
    the full,*
Just and Holy God, you are with us.

Another Way

1. Have someone hold up a star at the start of each section and move to one of the four corners of the church as each section is offered.

2. Sing one verse of the carol *The First Nowell* (*Voices United* #91) before the prayer and after each section.

3. Sing *Hope Shines as a Solitary Star* (*More Voices* #220) after each section.

4. Use the theme of having a journey to make.

As global citizens committed to justice, we have a journey to make.
To work for a world where political leaders see beyond
    narrow national interests.

To work for a world where terrorists are denied a homeland.
To work for a world where peaceful protest does not meet
with violent response.
To strive for a country where no child goes to school hungry.
To strive for a neighbourhood where each elderly person is
respected.
To ensure that our town/city is one where food banks and
sheltered housing are available,
and no one is left outside hungry in the cold.
Just and Holy God,
the star sign is our call to get involved.

*As those who are searching for the relief of suffering, we
have a journey to make.*
Our journey will call us to give a break to those whose routine
is relentless.
Our journey will show us those with emotional challenges and
enable us to listen to them.
Our journey will call us to advocate for the oldest, the
youngest, and the most vulnerable.
Our journey will take us to those who suffer pain and loss,
and enable us to comfort them.
Our journey will enable us to encourage the medical and
support staff in homes and hospitals.
Our journeying will prepare us to speak hopeful words to
those who are depressed or fearful.
We pray for those within our families or our church family
who sick or bereaved *(time of silent reflection)*.
Just and Holy God,
the star sign is our call to get involved.

*As members of the faith community, we have a journey to
make. On that journey,*
we will respond to the call to discipleship in fresh ways;
we will review old traditions and explore new paths;
we will be alert to unforeseen avenues of Christian service
and go there;
we will value afresh the gifts of our brothers and sisters in
Christ.
Just and Holy God,
the star sign is our call to get involved.

As those loved by God, we have a journey to make.
We will journey eagerly and leave in the past failures that have
compromised our self-esteem.
We will be ready to review those areas of life that trouble us.
We will be willing to try new leisure and work activities and
live with challenges that arise.
We will be determined to search out new friends or friendship
groups and face our feelings of vulnerability *(time of silent
reflection)*.
**In every effort we make to use our talents and abilities to
the full,**
Just and Holy God you will be with us.

1st Sunday after the Epiphany
Baptism of the Lord

LECTIONARY READINGS
Isaiah 42:1–9
Psalm 29
Acts 10:34–43
Matthew 3:13–17

*Jesus is singled out for ministry by John the Baptizer,
and is anointed by the Spirit.*

*Jesus was baptized by John and his ministry began. We too
are called to minister to our world:*
to gain the confidence of elected leaders in our area;
to speak out directly against racial slurs, "jokes," or prejudiced
remarks;
to learn about the threats to our environment and to advocate
for change;
to be alert to the needs of the poorest on our planet and find
ways to meet their needs;
to be aware of those at risk in our neighbourhood and find
ways of helping them.
*Sometimes we see ministry as work that other people do.
Loving God, you call each one of us to minister.*
We will minister.

*Jesus was baptized by John and his ministry began. We too
are called to minister to those who suffer.*
We will minister to those who find it difficult to share, and to
those who find it difficult to limit their sharing.
We will minister to those who are challenged by schoolwork
or by bullying.
We will minister to those who feel ill but are frightened of
going to the doctor.
We will minister to those who have a condition that does not
respond to treatment.
We will minister to those who have suffered loss – of a friend, a
loved one, a marriage or committed relationship, good health, a
cherished hope for the future. And we will minister to those who
will not accept the reality of their loss *(time of silent reflection)*.

Sometimes we see ministry as work that other people do.
Loving God, you call each one of us to minister.
We will minister.

Jesus was baptized by John and his ministry began. We too are
called to minister to our faith community, our church:
to support those who work quietly yet effectively in the
background;
to pray for those who lead worship, give leadership, and pastorally care for the members here *(time of silent reflection)*;
to encourage participation in the worldwide work of the
church through mission funds;
to find an area of service in the local congregation and
enthusiastically work within it;
to deepen our faith through learning and use our new-found
knowledge to encourage service.
Sometimes we see ministry as work that other people do.
Loving God, you call each one of us to minister.
We will minister.

Jesus was baptized by John and his ministry began. We too
are called to minister
to our family and friendship circles and to our own needs;
to stand beside those who have encountered a perfect storm of
trouble this week;
to have the wisdom to leave the past in the past;
to find common ground with those who see life differently
from us;
to dream of new places to go and new things to do with those
closest to us;
to freely give ourselves the time we need for enjoyment – for
listening to and making music, for laughing and playing with
children, and for cultivating and smelling the roses.
We will minister, Loving God, and we will be ready to
receive ministry.

Another Way

1. After each section, a member of the congregation might speak
   of the church's ministry to the world, the suffering, and the faith
   community, or of their own experience of being ministered to.

2. **Use a prayer with more silence to allow the congregation to pause and reflect.**

Jesus was baptized by John and his ministry began. We too are
called to minister to our world:
to gain the confidence of elected leaders in our area.
(Time of reflection.)
to learn about the threats to our environment and to advocate
for change.
(Time of reflection.)
to be alert to the needs of the poorest on our planet and find
ways to meet their needs.
(Time of reflection.)
to be aware of those at risk in our neighbourhood and find
ways of helping them.
(Time of reflection.)
Sometimes we see ministry as work that other people do.
Loving God, you call each one of us to ministry.
We will minister.

Follow the same pattern for the other sections.

3. **At the end of each section, water may be poured into the baptismal font from a pitcher. Or the congregation may be lightly sprayed with water from a frond or leafy branch.**

2nd Sunday after the Epiphany

LECTIONARY READINGS
Isaiah 49:1–7
Psalm 40:1–11
1 Corinthians 1:1–9
John 1:29–42

*The significance of Jesus is confirmed by the Spirit.
Jesus is with those who join him in God's work.*

***Jesus was chosen for a purpose; the disciples were chosen
for a purpose. God has a purpose for our world.***
Our Creator God wants our world to be one where women
    and children are honoured and respected.
Our Just God wants the developed countries to share with
    those that lack food, resources, and economic muscle.
Our Merciful God wants justice to overcome corruption and fear.
Our Friendly God wants those who are healthy and active in commu-
    nity to band together to support the downtrodden and oppressed.
What purpose has God in mind for us as we look around at
    our local community and the rest of the world? *(Time of
    silent reflection.)*
**God calls us
to work out God's purpose prayerfully and practically.**

***Jesus was chosen for a purpose; the disciples were chosen
for a purpose. And God's loving purpose goes to work
within the pain that God feels deeply.***
Our compassionate God sees those bound with invisible
    chains, and wants them to break free.
Our compassionate God sees the disturbed and disadvantaged
    and wants them to have the resources they deserve.
Our compassionate God sees those who feel ill at ease in their
    jobs and desires stability and fulfillment for them.
Our compassionate God sees those for whom illness never
    seems to end and desires peace with the uncertainty.
Our compassionate God sees friends and family members
    going through the desolate place of bereavement and knows
    a comforter is needed.
What purpose has God in mind for us as we look at our loved
    ones and our local community needs? *(Time of silent reflection.)*

God calls us
to work out God's purpose prayerfully and practically.

Jesus was chosen for a purpose; the disciples were chosen
for a purpose.
God has a purpose for God's church.
The Founder of the church sees community activities that
provide alternatives to church and poses the question, "Are
church activities and programs well founded?"
The Head of the church knows that the realm of God needs
committed and visionary persons to work out its values and
leadership, and poses the question, "Can you help?"
The Inspirer of the church reminds us that it is through
learning and prayer that we grow as persons of faith, and
poses the question, "In which areas will you grow?"
The Holy One who chose Jesus shows us that there is
relevance in the gospel that resonates today, and poses the
question, "How will you serve faithfully?"
God calls us
to work out God's purpose prayerfully and practically.

Jesus was chosen for a purpose; the disciples were chosen
for a purpose. God has a purpose for each one of us.
Is it to share our faith with well-loved family and friends?
Is it to share our faith with those we meet by chance?
Is it to review our life's direction, and our relationships?
Is it to venture out into fresh arenas of faith and service?
Is it to find ways of working with others with the compassion
and dedication of Jesus?
Is it to respond to God's calling? *(Time of silent reflection.)*
Each one of us is called to work out God's purpose
prayerfully and practically.

Another Way

1. Before the prayer a member of the congregation might speak
   about her/his purpose as one who has Christian faith, and
   how that faith influences different aspects of her/his daily life.

2. After each section, sing the first verse of *Arise, Your Light*
   Is Come (*Voices United* #79) or the chorus of *Go Make a*
   Diff'rence (*More Voices* #209).

3rd Sunday after the Epiphany

LECTIONARY READINGS
Isaiah 9:1–4
Psalm 27:1, 4–9
1 Corinthians 1:10–18
Matthew 4:12–23

The people who lived in darkness have seen a great light.

Jesus brought light to our world, and we are the light-bringing followers of Jesus.
There is the darkness of poverty, disease, and the exploitation
of women and children.
There is the darkness of fear – among refugees, illegal
immigrants, and those fleeing an agonizing domestic situation.
There is the darkness of despair among economic outcasts and
those who are at risk of injury in the workplace.
There is the darkness of *(mention a current situation).*
We are bringers of the Christ light,
the light of peaceful change that can never be extinguished.

*Jesus brought light to the downhearted, and we are the
light-bringing followers of Jesus.*
There are persons known to us who are in conflict with
co-workers and fellow members of social groups.
There are members of our family who are struggling with
financial problems and a lack of confidence.
There are friends of ours who are ill, at home and in hospital.
There are members of this faith community who are feeling
the loss of loved ones in the deepest part of their being.
There are well-loved caregivers who do not know how they
will face tomorrow.
(Time of silent reflection.)
We are bringers of the Christ light,
the light of peaceful change that can never be extinguished.

Jesus brought light to his disciples, and we are the light-bringing followers of Jesus.
Some church members find it easier to hold on to yesterday
than to vision for a faithful tomorrow.

Some church leaders will not interact with the wider faith
community, Christian or non-Christian.
Some church worshippers are stuck fast in their habitual way
of worship.
Some church workers will not stand with the disheartened
and downtrodden.
We are bringers of the Christ light,
the light of peaceful change that can never be extinguished.

 *Jesus brought light to his disciples, and we are the
enlightened followers of Jesus.*
The light of the Christ will clearly show the way for us.
The light of the Christ will challenge us to persevere.
The light of the Christ will enable us to learn from our mistakes.
The light of the Christ will illuminate the hidden talents of
our friends.
The light of the Christ will turn us from apathy to action.
We are bringers of the Christ light,
the light of peaceful change that can never be extinguished.

Another way

1. Four members of the congregation come to the front of the
    church. Each holds a candle and places it on the Communion
    table. The first person offers the world section of the prayer,
    saying, "I light this candle for women and children who are
    being exploited, refugees, those who live in fear for their
    lives, those who are economically at risk, and those who
    (current situation)." There is then a time of silence.

    The second person offers the suffering section, saying, "I
    light this candle for those who are ill, have financial problems,
    are mourning the loss of a loved one, and for stressed
    caregivers." Then there is a time of silence.

    Follow this pattern for the church and personal sections.

2. Sing one of the hymns of light from the Epiphany section of
    the hymn book. One appropriate hymn is *Will You Come and
    See the Light* (*Voices United* #96). After each section of the
    prayer, sing a verse of the hymn.

4th Sunday after the Epiphany

LECTIONARY READINGS
Micah 6:1–8
Psalm 15
1 Corinthians 1:18–31
Matthew 5:1–12

Then he began to speak and taught them, saying, "Blessed."

God blesses all the people in the world.
Blessed are the leaders of developed nations who pass up a
chance to exploit developing nations and share with them
instead.
Blessed are the peacemakers who persist when their friends
say, "Conflict is inevitable."
Blessed are the physically and mentally challenged who
celebrate their abilities in the workplace and with their
families, and blessed are those who support them.
Blessed are those who struggle to earn enough money for their
family to survive.
Blessed are the victims of abuse who find a way of making
their situation known.
And blessed are those who stand with them.
Following the pattern of Jesus, God's Holy One,
we share in God's blessing.

God blesses the powerless and overlooked.
Blessed are those who refuse to give in to self-pity when
surprised by sickness.
Blessed are the medical support staff members, for their work
is crucial yet often not visible.
Blessed are those addicted to drugs, alcohol, or food who are
open about their addictions, and blessed are those who
struggle in secret.
Blessed are the dying who find peace at the end of their time,
and blessed are those for whom the end of this life is slow
agony.
Blessed are those who find it a joy to help their ailing loved
ones, and blessed are those for whom it is a harrowing
experience.

Blessed are those who have suffered loss who find someone to
  listen deeply to them.
We pray for those we know *(time of silent reflection)*.
Following the pattern of Jesus, God's Holy One,
we share in God's blessing.

God blesses people in the church.
Blessed are the church leaders who joyfully commit time and
  personal skills to the faith community.
Blessed are those who find time for a job that must be done.
Blessed are the pastoral caregivers who sit beside the lonely
  and eat with the despised.
Blessed are those with a global vision who support the
  underprivileged and those without hope as if they were next
  door neighbours.
Following the pattern of Jesus, God's Holy One,
we share in God's blessing.

And God blesses each one of us.
We are blessed with the gift of life and God's unlimited gifts to us.
We are blessed as we return the smile of a child.
We are blessed by the wise words of an older person who is
  our friend.
We are blessed by the frosty wonder of a winter's day.
We are blessed by having caring family members and good friends.
We are blessed by the assurance and challenge of our Christian
  faith.
Following the pattern of Jesus, God's Holy One,
we share in God's blessing.

Another Way

1. Personal testimony would be helpful here. If there is a
   physically challenged person in your congregation, he/she
   might speak of how he/she is blessed.

2. For the personal section, the leader or another might speak of
   his/her blessings, starting with, "I am blessed with ___" and at
   the end say, " In silence, think of how you are blessed."

3. Sing the refrain of *Blest Are They* (*Voices United* #896) after
   each prayer section.

5th Sunday after the Epiphany

LECTIONARY READINGS
Isaiah 58:1–9a (9b–12)
Psalm 112:1–9 (10)
1 Corinthians 2:1–12 (13–16)
Matthew 5:13–20

> *You are the light of the world. Let your light shine.*

Into the darkness of the world, the light of Jesus Christ comes.

Into the hard place of struggle with computers and new technologies comes the kindly guide to solve problems.

Into the hard place of the prison cell comes a visitor who gives the light of new insights and hope.

Into the village where women have to walk miles to get fresh water comes the gift of a simple water pump.

Into the home where one parent is juggling a full-time job with care for young children comes the support of friends and neighbours.

We are light-bringers.

We support those who bring light in the way of Jesus Christ.

Into the dark places of suffering, the light of Jesus Christ comes.

Where an accident in the home or on the highway has caused tension, new realities are faced.

Where health professionals struggle to find out what is wrong with a patient, there is persistence.

Where memory loss increases, there is a readiness to deal practically with daily living.

Where loneliness has become a nagging pain, there is a reaching out to groups of friendly people.

Where a loved one has died, there is all the necessary time to come to terms with loss, and to grieve.

We are light-bringers.

We support those who bring light in the way of Jesus Christ.

Into the dark places of the church, the light of Jesus Christ comes.

Where the divide between age groups is clear, there are shared meals and conversations that bring understanding.

Where there is resistance to the future, or to working out a vision, there are new ideas and fresh enthusiasm.

Where there is reluctance to give for the work of the wider church, there is a new appreciation of what mission work is about.

We are light-bringers.

We support those who bring light in the way of Jesus Christ.

 Into the dark places of our own lives, the light of Jesus Christ comes.

Where we have lacked the will to take a decision, we now summon up the courage to move forward.

Where we have been troubled by a breakdown in relationship, we now search out the cause and work thoroughly to restore good feelings.

Where we have been apathetic and uncaring, we now work to become focused and motivated again.

We are the light-bringers of Jesus Christ, and we need the light of Christ in ourselves.

Another Way

1. At the start of each section a different source of light might be lifted up: flashlight, barbeque lighter, matches, key chain light, Christmas lights, etc. (anything but a candle!).

2. Base the prayer on Matthew 5:13, "You are the salt of the earth..." This is a well-known phrase meaning those who are most compassionate, just, kind, and forgiving.

 A simple prayer with silence.

Who are the salt of the earth? The salt of this world?

The salt of the earth stand beside those who struggle with the computer revolution.

The salt of the earth stand beside prisoners, refugees, and
strangers at risk.

The salt of the earth stand beside those at risk in our
community – the homeless, those who cannot feed their
children breakfast.

The salt of the earth support one-parent families.

How can we help them? *(Time of silent reflection.)*

**Who are the salt of the earth? Who are the "salty"
compassionate ones?**

The salt of the earth accept the mentally sick for who they are.

The salt of the earth care for elderly parents and accept
children into their homes after school.

The salt of the earth support those who mourn and those who
are dying.

How can we help them? *(Time of silent reflection.)*

**Who are the salt of the earth? Who are the salt of the
church?**

The salt of the church do the menial but essential jobs without
seeking notice.

The salt of the church volunteer for leadership tasks even
though they are already busy.

The salt of the church have broad horizons which include the
wider groups of church and mission.

How can we help them? *(Time of silent reflection.)*

Can we be included with the salty ones?

What opportunities are there right now for us to join the
ranks of the salty?

In our homes and family circles?

In our fraternal and sports groups?

Among those who seek justice through peaceful protest?

In our faith community?

Are we called to be salt of the earth people? *(Time of silent
reflection.)*

6th Sunday after the Epiphany
Proper 1

*If this is the Sunday before Ash Wednesday, this Proper may be
replaced by the readings for the Last Sunday after the Epiphany in
those churches using Transfiguration readings on this day.*

LECTIONARY READINGS
Deuteronomy 30:15–20
Psalm 119:1–8
1 Corinthians 3:1–9
Matthew 5:21–37

Choose the life that is fulfilling and forgiving.

There are choices to be made in our world, Living God:
to support those who bring humankind together for the study of
HIV/AIDS, and to advance the cause of peace on the planet;
to listen carefully to the ethical questions around the
growing of replacement organs and the challenging field of
reproductive technology;
to see the whole of humankind as our brothers and sisters,
and to welcome the refugee and stranger;
to pray for our leaders and local representatives *(insert names)*
and to recognize opportunities to play an active part in
political life.
Where there are hard choices to be made,
we are prepared to play our part.

There are choices to be made about those going through
hard times:
to provide a place where those who cannot work can meet and
share frustrations and find ways forward;
to stand beside those who have neither the strength nor the
will to go on;
to recognize the dignity denying aspects and the separation
from loved ones that come with hospital life;
to take the time that is needed to support those who have
long-term problems.

We pray for those who cannot work through injury or because there is no job available.

We pray for those we know who are struggling with physical illness.

We pray for those we know who are struggling with mental illness.

We pray for those who are facing the end of life.

We pray for those who are bereaved *(time of silent reflection)*.

Where there are hard choices to be made,
we are prepared to play our part.

There are choices to be made in the church:
to invite into our space local youth organizations, community and seniors' groups;

to joyfully welcome the stranger and newcomer to the neighbourhood;

to say words of encouragement and thanks to the persons whose work we take for granted;

to listen carefully for what Christian churches can do together and what we can do as one faith group with other faith communities.

Where there are hard choices to be made,
we are prepared to play our part.

Each of us has to make choices:
to curb our impatience, when we see a job that we think needs doing right away;

to be ready to forgive, even when we have been hurt badly and feel like harbouring a grudge;

to balance our home life with those activities we enjoy outside the home.

to be ready to venture into new areas of learning and to try out weight training, walking, swimming, or other physical activities.

In order to make important life changes, we know there are choices to be made.

Another Way

1. **There could be a preface to the prayer that makes it clear that there are choices to be made in every part of life: which**

clothes to wear, what to eat or cook, which charity to donate to, etc. These choices could be mimed before the spoken prayer is offered.

---

2. Prayer of Forgiveness

 In spite of corruption in high places,
Forgiveness.
In spite of government employees treating members of the
   public carelessly,
in spite of people like you and me treating government
   employees carelessly,
Forgiveness.
In spite of job discrimination against qualified immigrants,
Forgiveness.
In spite of the poor treatment of whistleblowers,
Forgiveness.
In spite of the unfairness and cruelty of our world,
Forgiveness,
and the seed of a new way.

 In spite of impatience with the careless and lazy,
Forgiveness.
In spite of the indifference of some caregivers,
Forgiveness.
In spite of the unreasonable demands of some patients,
Forgiveness.
In spite of harsh words said when pain was at its height,
Forgiveness.
In spite of failure to realize that a dying patient hears but
   cannot respond,
Forgiveness.

Carry on in this format for the rest of the sections.

7th Sunday after the Epiphany
Proper 2

*If this is the Sunday before Ash Wednesday, this Proper may be
replaced by the readings for the Last Sunday after the Epiphany in
those churches using Transfiguration readings on this day.*

LECTIONARY READINGS
Leviticus 19:1–2, 9–18
Psalm 119:33–40
1 Corinthians 3:10–11, 16–23
Matthew 5:38–48

Live generously, give generously.

**You call for our attitude to our world to be big-hearted, not
small-minded,**
so that the challenging work of police officers and security
personnel is appreciated and those serving with the military
overseas are not forgotten;
so that international aid-givers forgive loans and help children
and women at risk directly;
so that the plight of political prisoners is widely known;
so that small business owners are encouraged and grants that
enable persons to find useful work are given.
**O God you have given us so much,
enable us to share generously in return.**

**You call for our attitude to the suffering to be big-hearted,
not small-minded,**
so that the lazy, careless, and indifferent might be understood
and not written off;
so that treatment and drugs may be given and received
without anxiety about the cost;
so that the necessary equipment is available for diagnosis, and
a home away from home is available for the sick and their
loved ones;
so that the depressed may be noticed, and the anguish of those
with memory loss may be heard;

so that those who have suffered loss of a life partner through death or divorce may be comforted.

We pray for those we know who are sick, bereaved, or going through hard times *(time of silent reflection)*.

O God, you have given us so much,
enable us to share generously in return.

You call for our attitude within the faith community to be big-hearted, not small-minded,

so that the musicians, actors, and writers will be encouraged and their talents put to work;

so that cleaners, teachers, bookkeepers, coffee makers, and social activists will be encouraged and their talents put to work;

so that children will be listened to, and their opinions and needs taken seriously;

so that leaders will be thoroughly trained and their workload carefully monitored;

so that the work of the wider church will be carefully financed and seen as vital;

so that the traditions of other faiths will be studied and their scriptures seen as revealing divine truth and challenge.

O God, you have given us so much,
enable us to share generously in return.

You call for each one of us to be big-hearted, not small-minded.

Enable us to be realistic in our expectations of others, and understanding when they don't do things our way.

Enable us to listen carefully to the needs of those close to us and respond with sensitivity.

Enable us to consider our gifts and skills carefully, and fit them with community needs.

Enable us to accept the words, "You have done more than enough, it's time to take a break."

Broaden our horizons so that we feel able to help those in need beyond our borders.

As we consider your gifts to us, O Most Loving God, we give thanks through our gifts to others.

Another Way

1. Before the prayer, ask each person in the congregation to give something to another person sitting near them (not a family member) as a symbolic act of generosity (e.g., a coin, a thought, a greeting, a look at a photo of children or grandchildren, a smile).

2. The whole prayer is printed in the bulletin and congregants silently read the phrases. No spoken words by congregational members.

You call for attitude that is big-hearted, not small-minded, within each one of us. (Hold silence for 45–60 seconds, while congregants read the following phrases.)

read in
silence
Enable us to carefully listen to the needs of those close to us and respond with sensitivity.

Enable us to consider our gifts and skills carefully, and fit them with community needs.

Enable us to accept what we hear when someone whom we respect says, "You have done more than enough."

Broaden our horizons so that we feel able to help needs beyond our borders.

As we consider your gifts to us, O Most Loving God, we will give thanks through our gifts to others.

Carry on in this format for the other sections.

8th Sunday after the Epiphany
Proper 3

If this is the Sunday before Ash Wednesday, this Proper can be replaced by the readings for the Last Sunday after the Epiphany in those churches using Transfiguration readings on this day.

LECTIONARY READINGS
Isaiah 49:8–16a
Psalm 131
1 Corinthians 4:1–5
Matthew 6:24–34

Don't be concerned about the necessities of life, be concerned with God and God's Kingdom and God will provide.

Your world is so wonderful, God, Creator beyond imagining. The towering mountains, the fast flowing streams, the wildflowers, the variety of animals and birds – every fresh, glowing image of your creation is a cause for thanksgiving.

The world is wonderful, but we worry.

We worry about the abuse of land and water, the streams that are not fit to drink or swim in, the land on which children cannot play; the bird, animal, and plant species threatened with extinction.

We worry about the children who go to bed hungry, and the elderly who are neglected and abused.

We worry about those who are unemployed and feel useless.

Loving God,
you call us to let our worries go, and support those who bring a change for good.

The human body is so wonderful, God, Creator beyond imagining.

We have the ability to walk and run, to grasp and hold, to eat and digest food, to smell new mown grass and hear the morning chorus of birdsong. There is the miracle of birth, a new baby finding her mother's breast. How are we to thank you for these gracious gifts?

The human body is wonderful, but we worry.

We worry when our body is tested and it fails us.

We worry when we have strains and aches and pains that take time and the skill of trained medical professionals to put right.

We worry when good friends and loved ones are seriously ill, and we feel helpless in the face of their incapacity.

We worry because not enough persons sign up as blood or organ donors.

We worry when loved ones are dying, and feel the emptiness of bereavement when they are gone.

We bring them before you in prayer, our compassionate God.
(Time of silent reflection.)

Loving God,

you call us to let our worries go, and support those who bring a change for good.

The Church is wonderful, God, Faith Community Builder beyond imagining.

Here we are able to worship among friends, yet we can be still and know you are our God. Here we are able to question our faith and grow in fresh knowledge and understanding.

Here the young are introduced to the faith, and those who have died are celebrated and their loss mourned. For the church, we continually thank you.

The Church is wonderful, but we worry.

We worry about how we can present church programs and Bible study as relevant in an increasingly secular society.

We worry about the difficulties of providing skilled leadership for the groups within our faith community.

We worry about providing worship that is in tune with the values and worldview of those who are young and those who are old.

We worry about being practically just and compassionate, as Jesus was just and compassionate.

Loving God,

you call us to let our worries go, and support those who bring a change for good.

And each one of us is a wonderful person, ever-present and loving God.

We rejoice in our family and friends. We are grateful for the work we have done, for the holidays we have enjoyed, and the new places we have seen. Our life has been a wonderful journey of experience and discovery, but we worry.

We worry about how our friends see us.

We worry about our own health and the health of our loved ones.

We worry about our lack of confidence to use gifts and talents.

We worry about our reluctance to share our money with those who lack the bare necessities of life.

We worry about our relationships and our difficulties in forgiving and starting anew.

Loving God, you call us to let our worries go. You call us to work, pray and change our world, our church, and ourselves to the Kingdom pattern Jesus made clear.

Another Way

1. **Tell people to take up a worried body position at the beginning of each section. Suggest they hunch over and make a concerned face. When the prayer reaches the final phrase, "You call us to let our worries go," suggest they straighten up and raise their arms up and outwards.**

2. **Use biblical phrases to anchor the prayer.**

Jesus said, "Look at the birds of the air, they neither sow nor reap, nor gather into barns."

Glory in the wonders of creation.

Areas of God's creation are threatened, so work to bring change.

Children come right out with their simple questions, and elders share their memories. Rejoice with them.

Some children and elders are abused, so work to bring change.

Jesus said, "Don't worry about what you will eat or drink. Is not life more than food, and the body more than clothing?"

Glory in the wonderful food that you eat and the freedom you have to walk, swim, and exercise.

There are harmful food additives and cancer-producing chemicals in your diet, so work to bring change.

Rejoice in the satisfaction that comes from the work that you do and from working with those alongside you.

There is unemployment and trouble in the workplace, so work to bring change.

Jesus said, "Can any of you by worrying add a single hour to your life?"

Glory in the soaring of your soul as you pray and praise and read the scriptures.

There is falling church attendance and disagreement about creeds and doctrines, so work to bring change.

Rejoice in those who are your friends in faith community.

There is a need for skilled leaders, and a need for openness to new ways, so work to bring change.

Jesus said, "Strive first for the Kingdom of God and God's righteousness."

Glory in your life at this moment. Appreciate the variety of gifts you have been given and the opportunities to nurture your family and serve fellow men and women.

Don't sweat the small stuff: the problems of the day, the challenges at home, at your social group, and your place of employment. Simply work to bring change.

Believe in yourself, for God is confident that you will be able to do God's work, vision God's Kingdom, and bring God's Kingdom closer. Work to bring change.

3. **Sing a verse of a "Kingdom" hymn or song, such as** *The Kingdom of God Is Justice and Peace and Joy* (*More Voices* **#146) or** *Seek Ye First the Kingdom of God* (*Voices United* **#356) at the end of the prayer.**

9th Sunday after the Epiphany
Proper 4

LECTIONARY READINGS
Deuteronomy 11:18–21, 26–28
Psalm 31:1–5, 19–24
Romans 1:16–17, 3:22b–28 (29–31)
Matthew 7:21–29

*Jesus makes the point that his words provide
a strong foundation.*

**You have much to teach us, O God. Your Word in the Bible
teaches us that your creation is good, and so we pray**
that recycling may be taken seriously the world over;
that farmland will be left without building development and
fertile for future generations.
Your word in the Bible speaks of peace,
that civilians may not be put at risk through warfare;
that those who encourage conquest and campaigns of terror
may be confronted;
that rivalry will be experienced on the sports field (or rink)
and not on the battlefield.
**And like the prophets of old,
God's Word encourages us to get involved where we are able.**

**You have much to teach us, O God. Your Word in the Bible
teaches us to show the compassion of Jesus Christ.**
And so we pray
for persons who find conflict between their own standards
and those that prevail in the workplace;
for each person who faces a health challenge;
for those who work in a situation where necessary resources
are in short supply, especially in the areas of nursing and
teaching;
for those in the hard place which is bereavement.
We remember those we know and care about *(time of silent
reflection)*.
**And like the disciples of Jesus,
God's Word encourages us to get involved where we are able.**

You have much to teach us, O God. Your Word in the Bible teaches us the value of friends.

And so we pray

that we may be sensitive to the lonely ones around us and invite them to eat and talk in our homes;

that we may be open to the friendship offered by others;

that we may nurture friendship within the church;

that we may make faith friends in other countries through our mission fund.

And like David and Jonathan, Ruth and Rachel, Paul and Barnabas, good friends who we read about in the Bible,
God's Word encourages us to get involved where we are able.

You have much to teach each one of us, O God. Your Word in the Bible reminds us to look to Jesus as an example. So we pray

for obedience when we are unexpectedly called to a new endeavour,

for confidence to express our dreams and to live them,

for courage when the way is tough,

for endurance in the hard places of life, for joy in each new day,

for a faith that questions and seeks the truth.

And like our forebears of the early church, Patrick, Francis, Catherine, and Christina, your Word encourages us to get involved where we are able.

Another Way

1. Sing the first verse of *Christ Is Made the Sure Foundation* (*Voices United* #325), before and after the prayer.

2. Or use silence to reflect on our foundations.

Foundations:

Good government,

care for children,

true and tested traditions,

respect for the elderly,

respect for the powerless.

Foundations for our country, foundations for our world.

(Time of silent reflection.)

Foundations:
Medical care without cost for each citizen,
encouragement for the lonely,
hope for those groups who are at a loss,
companionship for those passing through the valley of death.
Foundations the suffering may trust. *(Time of silent
reflection.)*

Foundations:
The Word of God, read and questioned;
the faith community, supporting and serving;
the church worldwide, joined in praise and caring.
Foundations of faith. *(Time of silent reflection.)*

Foundations:
Family and friends who are for us,
music that makes our spirit soar,
books and movies that inform us,
a spiritual life that inspires us,
a vision of God's Kingdom that is before us.
Foundations of our lives. *(Time of reflection.)*

---

3. **Pass Bibles through the congregation as the prayer is being
   offered. The Bibles may be marked at significant sections.**

Last Sunday after the Epiphany
Transfiguration Sunday

LECTIONARY READINGS

Exodus 24:12–18
Psalm 2 or Psalm 99
2 Peter 1:16–21
Matthew 17:1–9

*On the mountainside Jesus is transformed before the disciples'
eyes. Bathed in the light of God, he communes with Moses and
Elijah, two key figures in Hebrew history and legend. After this
incident, Jesus comes down from the mountain and is immediately
faced with a request to put right a mentally sick child.*

We ache for our world to be transformed, O God,
so that developed nations will give from their abundance
to those that are struggling. We think especially of *(insert
examples)*.
We ache for our world to be transformed, O God;
for the air to be purified so that visible haze and invisible
particles that eat away at the ozone layer will be no more.
We ache for our world to be transformed, O God,
so that children can no longer be abused by persons whom
they know well, or by predators on the Internet.
We ache for our world to be transformed, O God,
so that no child will go hungry, or lack a home.
In the acts of transformation,
we will play our part, O God.

We long for suffering to be transformed, O God:
for those scarred in childhood to be heard and supported;
for those who are fearful of their diagnosis or treatment to be
reassured;
for those who are sick to find hope *(we bring them to mind in
our prayer)*;
for those who know death is close to find peace;
for those who have lost a loved one to find comfort *(we bring
them to mind in prayer)*.
In the acts of transformation,
we will play our part, O God.

We yearn for the church to be transformed, O God:
to find inspired worship in new forms and patterns,
to have zest and enthusiasm take root in our faith community,
to venture out with other members to explain the purpose of
  church,
to find the motivation to look beyond our denomination and
  nation to serve the vulnerable of other churches and other
  countries.
In the acts of transformation,
we will play our part, O God.

 We strive to be transformed in heart and mind and spirit,
  O God:
to put self-doubt and pity behind us;
to realize our potential for encouraging others;
to find the strength to forgive those who have hurt us and
  the strength to say sorry to those whom we have treated
  shamefully;
to rejoice in our faith and to share it freely, practically,
  sensitively, and generously;
to believe beyond all doubt that in life, in the shadow of death,
  and when we say farewell to this life, your love is with us.
In our transformation,
you will play your part, O God.

Another Way

1. Before the prayer is offered, speak of the meaning of transformation. An object may look totally different when it is
   transformed. Flour and yeast become a crusty loaf of bread, a
   chrysalis becomes a butterfly. Open the hymn book to *Amazing Grace, How Sweet the Sound* (*Voices United* #266) and
   speak of the life transformation of John Newton that gave rise
   to the hymn. The Internet has several bios of John Newton
   that tell of his conversion/transformation experience as he
   steered a merchant ship through a huge storm: "Through many
   dangers, toils, and snares I have already come...."

2. Talk about the life of John Newton and sing the hymn
   Amazing Grace, How Sweet the Sound (*Voices United* #266).

3. Have a time of silent reflection after each section.

We yearn for the church to be transformed, O God,
to find inspired worship in new forms and patterns;
to have zest and enthusiasm take root in our faith community;
to find a mission to work joyfully with others;
to find the motivation to look beyond our denomination and
    nation, and serve the vulnerable of other churches and
    countries. *(Time of silent reflection.)*
**In the acts of transformation,
we will play our part, O God.**

*We strive to be transformed in heart and mind and spirit,
    O God:*
to put behind us self-doubt and pity;
to realize our potential for encouraging others;
to find the strength to forgive those who have hurt us, and
    the strength to say sorry to those whom we have treated
    shamefully;
to rejoice in our faith and to share it freely, practically,
    sensitively, and generously;
to believe beyond all doubt that in life, in the shadow of death,
    and when we say farewell to this life, your love is with us.
    (Time of silent reflection.)
**In our transformation,
you will play your part, O God.**

Carry on in this format for the other sections.

SEASON OF LENT
Lent 1

LECTIONARY READINGS
Genesis 2:15–17, 3:1–7
Psalm 32
Romans 5:12–19
Matthew 4:1–11

Jesus goes into the wilderness and is powerfully tempted.

 Temptation is a powerful force in our world, O God.
Politicians trade power and influence for money and services.
Crooked financiers find ways to swindle and cheat innocent people.
Government officials are corrupt in some countries, and the
   governments of developed nations share increasingly small
   amounts of national revenue with developing nations.
Some employers give jobs to friends rather than the best
   qualified applicants.
Temptation is a force to be reckoned with.
Jesus resisted that force. We are called on to do the same.

 ***Temptation is a powerful force among those who control
   the powerless, O God.***
Employers offer jobs that have the risk of injury and pay low
   wages to the unemployed.
Local authorities regard those who are mentally and physically
   challenged as a low priority for help.
The elderly infirm are ignored and their concerns not heard.
We pray for the powerless and for those we know who are
   sick or troubled. We pray for those who are dying and for
   the bereaved *(time of silent reflection)*.
Temptation is a force to be reckoned with.
Jesus resisted that force. We are called on to do the same.

 Temptation is a powerful force in the church, O God.
Community groups need help but it is easy to ignore the needs.
Long-time worshippers find it challenging to welcome and
   encourage newcomers.

Congregational members find it easier to stay with existing
forms of worship.

Talented members shy away from the work and stress that
leadership might bring.

Cautious members are reluctant to give to funds that offer
help beyond the local congregation.

Door to door outreach to the local neighbourhood is seen as
copying the more extreme sects.

Temptation is a force to be reckoned with.

Jesus resisted that force. We are called on to do the same.

Temptation is a powerful force for each one of us, O God.
It is so easy to give in to the impulse that satisfies for the
moment.

It is so easy to go for personal gain rather than the faithful way.

It is so easy to avoid the just but unpopular cause.

It is so easy to keep silent when direct, personal support is
clearly needed.

It is so easy to close our eyes to the truth and give in to the
convenient way.

It is so easy to speak clearly about one way, yet act differently.

Temptation is a force to be reckoned with.

Jesus resisted that force. We are called on to do the same.

Another Way

1. Offer a "temptation" vignette before the prayer. For example,
   the "tempter" offers one person a large slice of apple pie. She
   refuses, saying, "I am on a diet." The tempter says, "You love
   apple pie and it won't hurt this once." The tempted one walks
   away.

   Or the "tempter" flashes a wad of dollar bills and says,
   "I'll make it well worth your while to look the other way
   when our planning application shows a harmful effect on
   wildlife in the area." The tempted one takes the money.

2. Sing a verse of the hymn *Jesus, Tempted in the Desert* (*Voices
   United* #115) or *When We Are Tested* (*More Voices* #65) after
   each section of the prayer.

Lent 2

LECTIONARY READINGS

Genesis 12:1–4a
Psalm 121
Romans 4:1–5, 13–17
John 3:1–17 or Matthew 17:1–9

God loved the world so much…

 ***We believe that the needs of the world can be met in the
spirit of love.***
The love that exposes greed and exploitation.
The love that will not judge persons on the basis of racial origin.
The love that speaks out against cruel dictatorship and the
silencing of political prisoners.
The love that puts no limits on supporting the care of children
or the dignity of elders.
The love that does not let the despairing go.
We have seen that love in Jesus.
We will express that love as followers of the Christ.

 ***We believe that the needs of the suffering can be met in the
spirit of love.***
The love that listens to those who have received bad news this
week.
The love that stands with the sick as they face their symptoms.
The love that supports patients who are chronically ill.
The love that persists in the face of a terminal diagnosis.
The love that sees patient care as a vocation as well as a job.
The love that stands with the bereaved.
We remember those who are sick, and the bereaved *(time of
silent reflection)*.
We have seen that love in Jesus.
We will express that love as followers of the Christ.

 ***We believe that the church can have an impact for good in
the spirit of love.***
The love that gets involved in sexual and environmental issues.
The love that questions creed and scripture.
The love that supports the downhearted.

The love that confronts darkness and despair.
The love that moves through boundaries of nation or creed.
We have seen that love in Jesus.
We will express that love as followers of the Christ.

 We believe that each one of us can be renewed in the spirit of love.
The love that gives us courage to face the characteristics of our personality.
The love that enables us to work through our weaknesses.
The love that will not give up on a friend or family member.
The love that is ready to risk and adventure.
The love that reaches to God through doubt, despair, and difficulty.
We have seen that love in Jesus.
We will experience it as a follower of the Christ.

Another Way

1. Sing a verse of *In Loving Partnership We Come* (*Voices United* #603) after each section of the prayer.

2. Use a fully responsive format.

 We believe that each one of us can be renewed in the spirit of love.
The love that enables us to work through our weaknesses.
The love that will not give up on a friend or family. member.
The love that is ready to risk and adventure.
The love that reaches to God through doubt, despair, and difficulty.
We have seen that love in Jesus.
We will experience it as a follower of the Christ.

Lent 3

LECTIONARY READINGS

Exodus 17:1–7
Psalm 95
Romans 5:1–11
John 4:5–42

Those who drink the water I give them will never be thirsty.

After each prayer section, pour a small amount of water into one of four glasses on the Communion table. At the end of the prayer, offer them to members of the congregation to drink.

Give water to our thirsty world, O God.
You remind us that the water we use now will have to be re-used by our children and grandchildren.
You remind us that while we get clean water from the tap, some women in Africa have to walk miles to a source of water which may be polluted.
You remind us that television, print, and digital media satisfy our thirst for knowledge, information, and fresh opinions.
You remind us that hockey, soccer, swimming, and golf satisfy the thirst of many for enjoyable sports.
You remind us that the world is thirsty for justice, peace, and understanding *(cite local and international examples)*.
Living God, you satisfy thirst.
We will be partners in providing living water.

You slake the thirst of the suffering, O God.
You stand beside those who call out for water but whose needs are denied.
You sustain the nurses and care staff who provide the basic care for hospital and institutional patients.
You comfort those whose thirst is for attention, friendship, or recognition.
You stand beside those whose loss of mental or physical facility has left them in a drought of friendship.
You are strength to those whose loss of a loved one has left them parched for compassion.
People who now come to mind *(time of silent reflection)*.

Living God, you satisfy thirst.
We will be partners in providing living water.

You give the living water to our church, O God.
The water of baptism is here to embrace both children and
   adults into faith community.
The water, juice, tea, coffee, and potluck meals are symbols of
   welcome, fellowship, and friendship.
The mission projects that supply water pumps, irrigation, and
   storage tanks are a reminder that our giving to communities
   we will never visit can change and save lives.
Living God, you satisfy thirst.
We will be partners in providing living water.

You give the living water to each one of us, O God.
Our thirst for new life and direction is satisfied by your Word
   found in scripture and in the lives of the saints, known and
   unknown.
We drink at the well of good relationship and close friendship.
We rejoice in the compassionate work that leaves us thirsting
   but satisfied, for your love has been a part of it all.
And our thirst for true life in the Spirit has us learning,
   venturing, and risking.
Living God, you satisfy our thirst.
We will be partners in providing living water.

Another Way

1. **Sing a verse of** *Like a Healing Stream* **(***More Voices* **#144) after
   each section.**

2. **Dialogue with the congregation around what they and others
   thirst for, and determine how their thirsting may be slaked.**

You refresh a thirsty world, O God.
Do you think we have enough water in the world for the
   future generations?
**You remind us that the water that we use now will have
   to be re-used by our children and grandchildren.**
How might we advocate for more economical water use?

Have any of you been in rural Africa? Do you know what the
chief occupation of women is in Kenya or Tanzania?

**You remind us that while we get clean water from the
tap, some women in Africa have to walk miles to a
source of water which may be polluted.**

Are there ways in which we could support those who dig
wells?

Lent 4

LECTIONARY READINGS
1 Samuel 16:1–13
Psalm 23
Ephesians 5:8–14
John 9:1–41

One thing I know; once I was blind, and now I see.

You give us the insight we need for our world, Loving God.
You enable us to see the huge inequalities in income between
the poor in our country and the poor in India and Ethiopia.
You enable us to understand how the aboriginal peoples suffer
through government inaction, neglect, and prejudice.
You enable us to understand the constant struggle of those
who suffer from eating disorders.
You enable us to feel the anxiety of military personnel in
Afghanistan and the frustrations of those who work for
peace, and justice for women, in that country.
You show us the areas of need in our neighbourhood *(local examples)*.
Once we were blind; now we see.
Enable us to use our new vision to bring change.

You give us the insight we need for the suffering, Loving God.
It is difficult to feel the agony of a young person teased or
bullied, but we remember how it once was with us.
It is difficult to enter the daily suffering of those challenged by
mental and physical conditions, but we make the effort.
It is hard for us to believe those who tell us they have
contracted a sickness in the hospital, but we try.
It is difficult to come to terms with the news that a loved one
we thought healed is now dying, but we face that reality.
We pray for those of our own family and our church family who
are sick and those who are bereaved *(time of silent reflection)*.
Once we were blind; now we see.
Enable us to use our new vision to bring change.

You give us the insight we need for the church, Loving God.
You help us to understand that some can hardly wait for worship
to begin and some can hardly wait for worship to end.
You help us to be patient with those who are impatient for change.

You help us to listen to the wisdom of children as well as of
those of advanced years.
You help us see those who do the small but essential jobs in
our church as well as the leaders.
You help us to see the vital need for faith community life in an
increasingly materialistic world.
Once we were blind; now we see.
Enable us to use our new vision to bring change.

 You give each one of us the insight we need, Loving God.
We will recognize our apathy and get involved.
We will perceive our huge capacity to do good and make a start.
We will be willing to look carefully at our relationships and
make the changes that are needed.
We will recognize ourselves as spiritual beings and give time
to prayer and spiritual practice.
We will have the courage to act on the insights we receive for
justice and peace
through the words and example of Jesus and contemporary Christians.
Enable us, Loving God, to use our new vision to bring change.

Another Way

1. **Have four people sitting at the front of the church, all blindfolded. At the end of the petitions of each section, have one person
   remove the blindfold and say, "Once I was blind and now I see!"**

2. **Have a visually impaired person speak before the prayer.**

3. **Give your opinion about blindness at the start of the prayer,
   and modify the way you offer the prayer accordingly.**

 We never realized that we were visually impaired persons.
You enable us to understand how the aboriginal peoples suffer
through government inaction, neglect, and prejudice.
You enable us to understand the constant struggle of those
who suffer from eating disorders.
You enable us to feel the anxiety of military personnel in
Afghanistan and the frustrations of those who work for
peace, and justice for women, in that country.
Once we were blind; now we see.
Enable us to use our new vision to bring change.

Lent 5

LECTIONARY READINGS

Ezekiel 37:1–14
Psalm 130
Romans 8:6–11
John 11:1–45

> *It seemed as if there was death and yet Jesus
> saw there was life*

Symbols of life in the midst of death *could be useful here: buds on
"dead" branches (do you see the bare branch or the buds?); a brochure
for sunny countries attached to a snow shovel; a sun hat poking out of
a winter boot.*

It is easy to stay focused on the worst aspects of our world.
It is easy to see the huge numbers of people who cannot find
meaningful work, if any at all *(give local examples)*, and
miss seeing the initiatives that bring work and hope to the
unemployed.
It is easy to see the huge numbers of people in refugee camps
(give examples), desperate to find a permanent home,
and fail to notice the efforts of countries such as Canada,
Sweden, and Australia to accept and give a second chance to
those who have been uprooted from their homeland.
It is easy to see the destruction of the forests and the paving
over of good agricultural land *(use current examples)*, and
not notice the efforts of those who strive to keep land free of
urban development.
**Sometimes it seems that death and destruction will get
their way.**
**Yet Jesus saw that life was present in the darkness, and
so can we.**

It is easy to stay focused on the worst aspects of the suffering.
For some of us it is hard to get to sleep and stay asleep, yet for
others a sound sleep is taken for granted.
Many people are unable to get the drugs and treatment that
they need *(give local examples)*, yet for so many others
medical treatment is timely and compassionate.

Many parents are unable to get the help they need for their challenged children *(give local examples)*, yet others get wonderful help at home and at school.

Many family members are unable to get help for their dependent elderly relatives, yet there are others who enjoy wonderful home and institutional care.

Sometimes it seems that death and destruction will get their way.

Yet Jesus saw that life was present in the darkness, and so can we.

 It is easy to stay focused on the worst aspects of the church:

To be aware of conflict, division, and the lack of leadership and planning, and miss the faith communities that throb with life and faithfulness;

to be aware of faith communities that are inward looking and self-satisfied, and miss those churches that serve the local community and uphold the powerless *(give local examples)*;

to be aware of those faith communities that tell their members what they should believe,

and miss those churches that encourage their members to doubt, question, and learn *(give local examples)*.

Sometimes it seems that death and destruction will get their way.

Yet Jesus saw that life was present in the darkness and so can we.

 It is easy to stay focused on the worst aspects of ourselves:

To see ourselves as selfish and uncaring, and miss those aspects that make clear our generosity and compassion;

to see that part of ourselves that is reluctant to move forward and miss the part that is ready to journey into the unknown;

to see only our superficial and passing relationships and forget the good friends and caring family members who will always be there for us.

Sometimes it seems we dwell on the negative parts of our character, yet the life of Jesus calls us to accentuate the positive and find the life that is fulfilling and good.

Another Way

1. In the following prayer, we have not followed the theme of
the gospel reading but rather focused on the fact that it is
close to the end of Lent.

    The usual format of the prayer has been changed to
allow the specific petitions to be said by the congregation.
The leader may give the opening and closing phrases. If this
proves a problem in terms of taking too much space on the
bulletin, then the usual order may be restored.

The end of Lent. The road has been rough and hard for Jesus.
His purpose has been misunderstood.

Those who protest with signs, letters, lobbying, and marching
are misunderstood.

**Those who speak out for justice for the poor are
misunderstood.**

**Those who speak out against elder abuse are
misunderstood.**

**Those who work to end prejudice against racial
minorities are misunderstood.**

**Those who speak out against bullying in schools are
misunderstood.**

We are called to Christian solidarity with the misunderstood.

The end of Lent. The road has been rough and hard for Jesus.
He suffers the harsh words of his friends and persecution
from his enemies.

We think of those who are the victims of smear campaigns at
work or in their social groups.

**We remember those whose sickness or symptoms are not
taken seriously by family members, by friends or by
medical personnel.**

**We think of those for whom visiting is restricted by the
outbreak of disease.**

**We pray for all those having a hard time in hospitals and
those who are sick at home especially those who are
neglected by family and friends** (*time of silent reflection*)**.**

**We remember the bereaved; we think of those whose
loved ones have been killed in accidents; we think
especially of parents whose children have died; we**

**remember all those for whom the loss of a loved one
is so difficult to bear; and those who stay with them**
(time of silent reflection).
We are called to Christian solidarity with the suffering.

The end of Lent. The road has been rough and hard for Jesus.
He knows the Lenten road is the end of all that was good in
his human life.
**We are aware of persons who have come to an ending:
family members and friends who are at the end of life;
those facing unemployment and retirement; persons
at the end of a marriage or relationship; and those for
whom a dream has come to nothing.**
We are called to Christian solidarity with those who face an
ending.

 The end of Lent. The road has been rough and hard for Jesus.
And we face some rough journeys as well.
In our loneliness, travel with us, O God.
When nothing seems to go right, travel with us, O God.
**When loved ones and friends let us down, travel with
us, O God.**
When we travel the wrong road, travel with us, O God.
**When we give in to apathy or despair, travel with us,
O God.**
The God who stands ready to show each of us the right way,
the God of our endings as well as our beginnings, is in
solidarity with us.
Thanks be to God!

Lent 6
Palm/Passion Sunday

LECTIONARY READINGS
FOR THE LITURGY OF THE PALMS

Matthew 21:1–11
Psalm 118:1–2, 19–29

A Palm/Passion Reflection

There will be significant time left for silent reflection in this prayer.

The people in the crowd watch Jesus and the disciples as they come into Jerusalem.
They wonder how the power people and the military feel about this charismatic person who threatens to take over the centre of the political stage.
We pray for the powerless in our world: the hungry, the intimidated, and the exploited poor here and in countries far from here *(time of silent reflection)*.
We pray for the powerless in *(our city/town)*: those without homes, those without money.
We wonder how we might support them *(time of silent reflection)*.

Among the crowd are persons who have been helped and healed in body, mind, and spirit by God's Chosen One. There is joy in their hearts! But there are also those who realize Jesus is going to his death.
We pray for those who are working to prevent disease; those advocating fitness programs and healthy diets; persons pressing for checkups for breast and prostate cancer.
We pray for those who have received an unexpected and disturbing diagnosis; those who are suffering at home or in hospital; and those who are dying or bereaved.
We think especially of persons in our families and friends within our church. We wonder, in silence, how we might support them *(time of silent reflection)*.

There are members of the synagogue and temple in the crowd. They are wondering how this prophet with huge popular appeal will affect their faith community, its life and work.

We pray for those of other faith groups and wonder which teachings and writings we can make our own.

We pray for those who are searching out the spiritual needs of those outside the faith community and wonder how we might meet those needs.

We pray for those who are looking to the future of our church and wonder what we might do to support them.

We pray for leaders of our wider church groups *(names)*. and wonder if we have a part to play in them

We pray for those for whom the money from mission funds is a crucial matter, and wonder how we might further support them *(time of silent reflection)*.

There are individuals in the Palm Sunday crowd who have heard Jesus teach and have changed their lifestyle or life's direction. There are those who have heard his message and stories second-hand and have taken them to heart.

We pray for ourselves

as we consider our life's direction,

as we think about our job or social activities,

as we ponder our relationships,

as we wonder about our life in family and community,

as we think about our limited life span,

as we think about how our Christian faith affects all of our lives *(time of silent reflection)*.

We wonder how the coming of Jesus to confront the powerful ones of his time will impact our life and our time *(time of silent reflection)*.

Another Way

1. Sing *Open Our Hearts* (*More Voices* #21) before the prayer and after each verse.

2. Pose the questions, "Why did Jesus go to Jerusalem?" and "What does it mean to us?" before the prayer and after each verse.

Why did Jesus go to Jerusalem?
He went to show that naked power was not acceptable in God's sight. Neither the chief priests nor King Herod could have their selfish way.
And today it is not acceptable that some children go to bed hungry.
It is not acceptable that women are paid less than men for the same work.
It is not acceptable that those who expose corruption in the workplace are not protected.
It is not acceptable that affordable housing is a low priority in many cities worldwide *(time of silent reflection)*.

Why did Jesus go to Jerusalem?
He went to show that the poorest people of his time were suffering and that it was unjust.
There is no compassion when... *(time of silent reflection)*.

Why did Jesus go to Jerusalem?
He went in faithful obedience to God and stayed faithful when the cross was the only option. The disciples ran away.
Our discipleship calls us to... *(time of silent reflection)*.

Why did Jesus go to Jerusalem?
He recognized and accepted that he was God's chosen one and could do nothing else.
Time of silent reflection.

Holy Thursday

LECTIONARY READINGS

Exodus 12:1–4 (5–10), 11–14
Psalm 116:1–2, 12–19
1 Corinthians 11:23–26
John 13:1–17, 31b–35

Christ's glory is revealed in those who serve.

One person washing the feet of another at the front of the sanctuary would be a good way to make the serving concept clear. Alternatively, a bowl and towel might be raised at the end of each section as a symbol of service.

 Christ's glory is revealed in those who serve.
We remember those who serve with the spirit of Jesus Christ in our world.
Jesus was a peacemaker.
We think of those who are striving to forge lasting peace in the lands where Jesus walked and taught.
Jesus was a justice seeker.
We think of those denied simple justice: the poor of this and other countries, the refugees without hope of finding a homeland, abused women and children.
Jesus was an opponent of the evil ones.
We think of those who stand up to the power of drug peddling gangs, those who advocate for racial minorities, and those who battle companies that ignore environmental regulations.
We think of young persons bullied because of their sexual orientation.
We will care for the needy of our world
as servants of the Servant.

 Christ's glory is revealed in those who serve.
We remember those who serve the suffering in the spirit of Jesus Christ.
Jesus cared for the sick and made people whole again.
Those lacking in self-esteem and confidence;
those whom life has treated harshly and those who cannot find a purpose in life.

We pray for those who feel the dull ache of depression; for
those struggling with drug and alcohol addictions and the
support groups that stand with them.
We pray for those concerned about the results of medical tests,
those who can see no end to their illness, those who are dying
and those who help the dying prepare for the last journey.
There are persons who are on our hearts and minds *(time of
silent reflection)*.
Jesus cared for the bereaved.
We pray for persons who have recently lost loved ones, and
those for whom the ache of loneliness goes on and on
We pray for those who have lost the will to live
Jesus stood beside the downhearted.
(Time of silent reflection.)
**We will care for the suffering
as servants of the Servant.**

Christ's glory is revealed in those who serve.
We remember those who serve the church in the spirit of Jesus
Christ.
Jesus was committed to proclaiming God's glorious realm.
We recall those who work to extend the horizons of the church
to encompass the downtrodden, the poor, and the despised.
Jesus was not narrow and exclusive, but flexible and accepting.
We pray for those who strive to bring the different branches
of the Christian church closer, and those who proclaim the
various faith paths to the one God.
**Jesus knew the Word of God, recognized its value, and
shared its significance.**
We pray for those who search the Word for today's truth,
and those who bring it vividly alive in their lives. We think
especially of *(time of silent reflection)*.
**We will care for the church,
as servants of the Servant.**

**Christ's glory is revealed in those who serve, and
amazingly that includes us.**
Christ's joy was experienced among his circle of disciples.
We remember the fellowship and fulfillment we have created
and shared within our family and friendship groups.
**Christ felt frustration when the religious and political
leaders would not listen.**

We recall times when our own voice of reason and common
sense was not heard.

**Christ's message was that the love of God did not end with
death.**

We rejoice in our belief that God's love is eternally and
wonderfully alive.

We will experience God's all-embracing care
as servants of the Servant.

Another Way

1. Use *The Servant Song* (*Voices United* #595) creatively, weaving
   the hymn into the prayer as you think fit.

Good Friday

LECTIONARY READINGS

Isaiah 52:13—53:12
Psalm 22
Hebrews 10:16–25 or Hebrews 4:14–16; 5:7–9
John 18:1—19:42

We come to the cross.

Hammer a nail into the crossbeam of a wooden cross at the front of the church after each phrase.

We come to the cross *(hammer nail in).*
We look up *(hammer nail in).*
And Christ looks down on us *(hammer nail in).*

We come to the cross.
We look up.
We see the broken Christ,
and we pray for those broken in our world.
We pray for refugees who have fled from their homes and
communities.
We pray for boys forced to fight as soldiers, and girls forced
into prostitution.
We pray for those hated by their neighbours or bullied by their
peers.
We pray for those whose home life is hell.
We pray for those whose work life is hell.
We pray for those broken by addictions.
(Time of silent reflection.)
The God who feels pain deeply,
calls us to reflection and to action.

We come to the cross.
We look up.
We see the suffering Christ,
and we pray for those suffering in our communities.
For those dominated by a parent or other family member,
we pray.
For those dominated by debt, we pray.

For lonely persons who wish they had friends, we pray.

For abused gay persons and the neglected elderly, we pray.

For those we know who are sick, especially family members, friends,

and members of our faith community, we pray *(time of silent reflection)*.

For those who have lost loved ones, we pray *(time of silent reflection)*.

For those who have had to put dreams or hopes to one side, we pray.

We pray for the suffering, for the deeply troubled, for the distressed.

The God who feels pain deeply
calls us to reflection and to action.

We come to the cross.
   We look up.
     We see the abandoned Christ.

We bring to mind those whose friends have let them down.

We bring to mind those dominated and controlled by their fears.

We bring to mind the unemployed and rejected.

We bring to mind the unloved children.

We pray for those who feel abandoned and alone in our world.

(Time of silent reflection.)

The God who feels pain deeply
calls us to reflection and to action.

 We come to the cross.
   We look up.
     And Christ looks down on us.

We reflect on and feel his helplessness.

We are aware of the parts of us that are suffering.

We know how our faith is tested by adversity.

We are acutely conscious of our personal failings and fears.

We wish that our friends would be there for us.

We wish we could forget an incident that haunts us.

We reflect on our own needs.

(Time of silent reflection.)

The God who feels pain deeply
calls us to reflection and to action.

Another Way

1. Slow the whole prayer down and insert a time of silence after each phrase, perhaps reducing the number of phrases. Leader can speak the whole prayer, apart from the last line.

We come to the cross.
We look up.
We see the abandoned Christ.
(Time of silent reflection.)
We bring to mind those whose friends have let them down.
(Time of silent reflection.)
The God who feels pain deeply
calls us to reflection and to action.

SEASON OF EASTER
Easter Sunday

LECTIONARY READINGS
Acts 10:34–43 or Jeremiah 31:1–6
Psalm 118:1–2, 14–24
Colossians 3:1–4 or Acts 10:34–43
John 20:1–18 or Matthew 28:1–10

Jesus is not here. He is risen.

Jesus is not here. He is risen. Where will he be found?
There are world leaders frustrated because they cannot forge
    peace.
There is death and suffering among military personnel, members
    of the police force, and firefighters *(use current examples)*.
There is heartache and hopelessness among those who are
    unemployed or exploited at work.
There is despair and grief among those who have lost loved ones.
**Jesus is found among those in danger, the hopeless and
    despairing.**
In Christ's rising,
we find hope.

Jesus is not here. He is risen. Where will he be found?
We know persons who wish they could share laughter and a
    meal this holiday weekend.
We know those who wish they had a family of their own.
We know family members and friends who are sick and depressed.
We know people in our church who are going through a hard time.
We know neighbours and community members who are tested
    and troubled.
We know those who have lost loved ones *(time of silent reflection)*.
**Jesus is found among the suffering and those who care
    for them.**
Jesus is found supporting the bereaved.
In Christ's rising,
we find hope.

Jesus is not here. He is risen. Where will he be found?
We long for a church that participates in the struggles of the
world's powerless.
We long for a church that responds sensitively to the practical
and spiritual needs of the local community.
We long for a church that struggles with what the Christian
faith means and how it is worked out day by day.
We long for a church that cares as much for faith communities
that require help from mission funds as for their own
church.
Jesus is found among those who ask the hard questions.
Jesus is found among those willing to venture out in
faith.
In Christ's rising,
we find hope.

Jesus is not here. He is risen. Where will he be found?
In our efforts to stand beside the troubled,
in our conflicts that are difficult to work out,
in our struggles to help our family and neighbours,
in our willingness to break free from discouragement and
frustration, depression and apathy,
in our joy at overcoming the barriers that hold us back.
Jesus is found when we face our challenges, reminding
us that it is in *hope*, wonderful, eternal *hope*, that
Christ is risen. Amen.

Another Way

1. Sing the chorus of *Hey Now! Singing Hallelujah!* (*More Voices*
   #121) or one verse of *We Meet You, O Christ* (*Voices United*
   #183) after each section.

2. Have a couple of persons accompany the prayer with
   tambourine and drum, and another two or three give an
   enthusiastic Yeah! at the end of each section of the prayer.

Christ is risen!
Refugees will know the hope of resettlement *(drum roll and
tambourine rattle)*.

The unemployed will have hope of work or retraining *(drum roll and tambourine rattle)*.

Christ *is* risen! Hope is alive! *(drum roll and tambourine rattle, Yeah! Yeah!)*

Christ is risen!
Those we know who are ill will find peace in the midst of suffering *(drum roll and tambourine rattle)*.

Those who have lost loved ones will know companionship in their sorrow *(drum roll and tambourine rattle)*.

Christ *is* risen! Hope is alive! *(drum roll and tambourine rattle, Yeah! Yeah!)*

2nd Sunday of Easter

LECTIONARY READINGS

Acts 2:14a, 22–32
Psalm 16
1 Peter 1:3–9
John 20:19–31

The risen Christ is with the disciples

As the prayer is about to begin, a few dejected-and-unsure-looking people scattered throughout the congregation stand up. The leader exclaims, "Christ risen!" The dejected ones come to the front of the church (could be one at a time, after each verse) and stand looking elated with their hands raised towards an invisible person in their midst. They represent persons who have been changed.

The risen Christ challenges us to consider our troubled world.
The risen Christ calls on us to work with those who point to
    the inequalities on our planet:
the lack of a fair electoral system in many countries;
the lack of protection for refugees and the dispossessed;
the lack of food, clean water, and shelter for many in the
    developing world;
the lack of education for many children, the lack of medical
    care for babies and young mothers;
the lack of job training for adults, and meaningful work for
    so many.
Jesus is the hope of the ignored and abandoned.
Christ risen!
is the heartfelt sign of change.

**The risen Christ challenges us to consider the suffering
    ones among us:**
those for whom a new day is a fresh round of drudgery;
those who cannot get the medical treatment they need;
those whose mental illness is ignored;
those who are put down and belittled;
those who cannot get to see their loved ones as often as they
    wish *(time of silent reflection)*;

those who have lost a friend or family member through
distance, conflict, or death *(time of silent reflection)*.
We pray for our families, friends, and those who are a part of
our faith community *(time of silent reflection)*.
Jesus suffered, and understands pain.
Christ risen!
is the heartfelt sign of change.

 ***The risen Christ challenges us to think about our faith
community, our church:***
to share worship that touches feelings as well as the intellect;
to listen to those who speak of new patterns of ministry;
to work with those who see local mission as a common
responsibility;
to reach out and talk with our neighbouring church members;
to hear the needs, celebrate the joys, and support the
aspirations of the young people in our midst.
Jesus was the inspiration for his disciple family.
Christ risen!
is the heartfelt sign of change.

 The risen Christ challenges us to be good to ourselves:
to take the time we need to care for loved ones and friends;
to recognize our need for a time to relax and refresh after a
rough patch;
to hear the encouraging words that others speak to us, as well
as the criticism;
to accept the need to give gifts to ourselves as well as to be
generous to others;
to build up our spiritual health through prayer, praise, and the
reading of inspirational books.
Jesus took time for prayer and celebration.
Christ risen!
is the heartfelt sign of change.

Another Way

1. At the end of each section, sing *Jesus Christ Is Risen Today*
   (*Voices United* #155) or the chorus of *Hey Now! Singing
   Hallelujah!* (*More Voices* #121).

2. Or turn this into a fully responsive prayer.

The risen Christ challenges us to be good to ourselves:
**To take the time we need to care for loved ones and
    friends;**
to recognize our needs for a time to relax and refresh after a
    rough patch;
**to hear the encouraging words that others speak to us,
    as well as the criticism;**
to accept the need to give gifts to ourselves as well as to be
    generous to others;
**to build up our spiritual health through prayer, praise,
    and the reading of inspirational books.**
Jesus took time for prayer and celebration.
(shouted out) **Christ risen! is the heartfelt sign of change.**

3rd Sunday of Easter

LECTIONARY READINGS

Acts 2:14a, 36–41
Psalm 116:1–4, 12–19
1 Peter 1:17–23
Luke 24:13–25

> *Jesus was known in the breaking of bread and everything changed for the two disciples.*

At the end of each prayer section, a piece of bread or bun is broken and the two pieces held up with arms extended.

 Jesus will be known in our world.
Jesus will be known when there is a global plan to meet earthquakes, flooding, and other natural disasters.
Jesus will be known when the basic needs of children for food, housing, and education are met in rural Kenya and Ethiopia as well as in Paris and Sydney.
Jesus will be known when the budgets for peacemaking are as large as the military ones.
Jesus will be known when the poor and powerless are treated with dignity.
Jesus will be known *(contemporary examples).*
Jesus will be known,
when the eyes of the care-less are opened!

 Jesus will be known among those who are hard pressed.
In giving children time to create and play, Jesus will be known.
In stilling the fears of those who are frightened of flying or leaving home, Jesus will be known.
In the listening of ministers, counsellors, social workers, and medical personnel, Jesus will be known.
In the hope of the chronically sick, Jesus will be known.
In the continued presence of loved ones beside those who have suffered loss, Jesus will be known.
We pray for those known to us *(time of silent reflection).*
Jesus will be known,
when the eyes of the care-less are opened!

Jesus will be known in the community of faith.
Jesus will be known as we freely give of our talents with others.
Jesus will be known when the need to praise and thank God
    for all God has so graciously given is recognized by those
    outside the church.
Jesus will be known when the crying needs of the
    neighbourhood are recognized and met.
Jesus will be known as the local church makes its welcome
    warm, sensitive, and lasting.
Jesus will be known as members make the giving of gifts to
    the wider church and mission a vital part of their work.
Jesus will be known,
when the eyes of the care-less are opened!

Jesus will be known in each one of us.
When we speak out and act for the downhearted and dispos-
    sessed, Jesus will be known.
When we refuse to share gossip or scandal, Jesus will be
    known.
When we take time for prayer and nurturing our spiritual life,
    Jesus will be known.
When we recognize and help the stranger, Jesus will be known.
When we listen for the call of God and follow, Jesus will be
    known.
When we suffer for what is just and lovely and true, Jesus will
    be known.
Jesus will be known in each one of us,
**and God will open our eyes to his presence on our life's
    journey.**

Another Way

1. Sing the chorus of *Bread for the Journey* (*More Voices* #202)
   or from *One Bread, One Body* (*Voices United* #467) after each
   section.

2. After every one or two phrases, have the congregation say,
   Open our eyes to what we can do.

Jesus will be known in the community of faith.
Jesus will be known when the need to praise and thank God
for all we have been so graciously given is recognized by
those outside the church.
Open our eyes, God, to what *we* can do.
Jesus will be known when the crying needs of the
neighbourhood are recognized and met…
Open our eyes, God, to what *we* can do.

4th Sunday of Easter

LECTIONARY READINGS
Acts 2:42–47
Psalm 23
1 Peter 2:19–25
John 10:1–10

The Good and Compassionate Shepherd

Led by the Good and Compassionate Shepherd,
we are aware of the fear and anxiety of those who live in
terror stricken areas of our world *(current examples)*.
We are free to express our shock at the killing in *(current
examples)* and to express our sympathy to bereaved family
members.
We feel the horror of vulnerable and defenceless children
abused by their parents.
We know the anger and despair that arise after deaths caused
by alcohol and drug affected drivers.
Christ who leads us,
you are the inspiration for change.

Led by the Good and Compassionate Shepherd,
we stand beside those who have lost their job.
We empathize with those whose dreams have crumbled to dust.
We encourage people to donate organs for transplant.
We express our concern for the lack of key medical services.
We express our love and compassion for those who are sick
and speak out for more housing for the working poor.
We comfort the bereaved and stay with them.
We bring those we know, those we love, before God *(time of
silent reflection)*.
Christ who leads us,
you are the inspiration for change.

Led by the Good and Compassionate Shepherd,
we are a centre of peace and calm to gather in.
We ask the local community how we can best meet their needs.
We express our willingness to work and worship with other
denominations and other faith communities.

We see beyond the local horizon and support the projects of
our mission fund.
Christ who leads us,
you are the inspiration for change.

 Led by the Good and Compassionate Shepherd,
we gain confidence to speak out for change.
We are free to explore new and surprising ventures.
We are prepared to study the Bible critically and carefully.
We sense the way to thank a friend.
We appreciate and learn from our mistakes.
We rejoice in faith that is alive and questioning.
Christ who leads us,
you are the inspiration for change.

Another Way

1. Sing the first verse of *The King of Love* (*Voices United* #273)
   after each prayer section.

2. Focus on the phrase from the gospel reading, "I came that
   they may have life and have it abundantly."

 Abundant life
Where the nations who have so much share with those who
have so little.
Abundant life
Where the only battles that happen take place on the soccer
field or the ice rink.
Abundant life
Where those who are physically or mentally challenged find
opportunity in the workplace.
Abundant life
Where racial diversity in a community is encouraged and
celebrated.
Abundant life
Giving, and giving again, as God has given to us.

Abundant life
Where those who lose their job are able to retrain for a
   fulfilling occupation.
Abundant life
Where the depressed and downhearted get the support and
   understanding they need.
Abundant life
Where family caregivers are able to have time away from their
   responsibilities.
Abundant life
Where the sick are told everything they need to know about
   their condition.
Abundant life
Where the dying find peace and the bereaved have someone to
   stay beside them.
(Time of silent reflection.)
Abundant life,
Giving and giving again, as God has given to us.

5th Sunday of Easter

LECTIONARY READINGS
Acts 7:55–60
Psalm 31:1–5, 15–16
1 Peter 2:2–10
John 14:1–14

*Jesus makes clear to the disciples that he is
with them, and God is with him.*

You are faithfully with us, O God. You are with our world.
Among the nations where terror and revenge root and grow,
    you are the way of reconciliation and peace.
Among those who are in the midst of industrial strife, you are
    the will for justice, the glimmer of hope.
Among those who seek controls on the pollution of air and
    water, you are the spirit of endurance, the refusal to accept
    second best.
Among those who fear abuse and harm every day, you are the
    hope of radical change.
As we work to make your world a good world, a fair world,
in the spirit of Jesus,
you call us to faithfulness.

***You are faithfully with us, O God. You are with us when we
    go through tough times,***
giving teachers patience with students who are disruptive,
giving students the courage to question teachers when
    information is unclear,
giving a calm spirit to those struggling with tax forms,
giving patients the confidence to express what is on their
    mind to their doctor,
giving doctors the confidence to speak plainly to their patients,
giving the dying a loving presence and the words of peace,
giving the bereaved permission to take the time they need to grieve.
We remember those who are downhearted and at a loss today
    (time of silent reflection).
As we stand beside the tested and sorely tried,
in the spirit of Jesus,
you call us to faithfulness.

And you call us to faithfulness. You are faithfully with us,
O God. You are within the communities of which we are
a part:
as the needs of the young and seniors are served,
as funds are raised for those without food and clothes, and
those at risk,
as the concern for good diet and exercise is addressed.
as our local congregation looks to the challenges of the coming
· years,
as our national church considers new structures and new
directions,
as our town/city struggles to find a peaceful and prosperous
future,
as our neighbourhood faces the challenges of *(cite examples)*.
As we commit ourselves to working with others for Gospel values,
in the spirit of Jesus,
you call us to faithfulness.

And you call us to faithfulness. You are faithfully with
each one of us, O God, whatever our situation may be:
searching with us for the direction that will be in line with
our gifts and talents.
Calling us to the way of compassion and sustained caring;
reminding us that we have the ability to forgive and to apologize;
steadying us when the storms of life threaten to engulf and
overturn us;
giving us confidence when, in failure and setback, we beat up
on ourselves.
As in past days you called Abraham and Ruth, Paul and Mary
Magdalene, Jean Vanier and Martin Luther King,
in the spirit of Jesus,
you call us to faithfulness.

Another Way

1. **Have one person stand at the front of the church facing the**
congregation. After each section, have another person come
to the front and join her/him and take her/his hand. At the
end of the prayer have the group hold hands in a circle, facing
outwards.

2. Focus on the words, *Jesus is the way*.

Jesus is the way.
Jesus is the way for those who struggle in the world:
> forgotten political prisoners, the working poor, those who
> > cannot get education, those who do not know where the
> > next meal is coming from.

(Time of silent reflection.)
Jesus is the way.
Jesus struggled and won through.

Jesus is the way.
Jesus is the way for those who suffer in the world:
> freedom seekers in one-party states, those whose illness is not
> > taken seriously,

(Time of silent reflection.)
Jesus is the way.
Jesus suffered and won through.

Jesus is the way.
Jesus is the way for today's faithful ones:
> those persecuted for what they believe, disciples whose
> > compassionate actions are challenged, churches that refuse
> > to remain cozy religious clubs.

(Time of silent reflection.)
Jesus is the way.
Jesus remained faithful and won through.

Jesus is the way.
Jesus had a rough time but did not waver.
Jesus is the way for each one of us.
In our doubt, he encourages us to question.
In our testing times, his example is strength.
In our discouragement, he encourages us to persevere.
(Time of silent reflection.)
Jesus is the way.
Jesus had a rough time but won through.

6th Sunday of Easter

LECTIONARY READINGS

Acts 17:22–31
Psalm 66:8–20
1 Peter 3:13–22
John 14:15–21

This Sunday celebrated as Christian Family Sunday.

Have the generations of one family offer this prayer, one member offering each section.

We realize, O God, that we are members of the worldwide family.

Where there is injustice, where children go hungry, and people of advanced years are neglected, bring insight and action.

Where there is conflict, where innocent civilians suffer, where fear reigns, where military persons abuse their power, bring reconciliation and lasting peace.

Where hope seems dead, when the downtrodden cry, "What's the use?" and corruption is an accepted part of the system, bring change and new ways.

Where there is need in the local community *(cite examples)*, bring change.

As members of the worldwide family, as members of the local community, as members of the family,
enable us to realize our responsibilities and our opportunities.

We realize, O God, that we are each a member of a cherished human family.

As we try to understand family members of a different age, personality, and generation from ourselves, give us empathy.

In our efforts to face family conflicts and to overcome longstanding grudges, give us courage.

As we stand beside the sick and listen to those who are in crisis and despair, give us patience.

As we are called on to lend a hand to the struggling, comfort the bereaved, and stay with those who have suffered loss, give us the endurance we need *(time of silent reflection)*.

We pray for family members, known and unknown. In a time
of silence, we celebrate their joys, remember their challenges
and offer our love to them *(time of silent reflection)*.
*As members of a particular human family, as members of
the family,*
**enable us to realize our responsibilities and our
opportunities.**

*We realize, O God, that we are members of the church
family.*
Before we enter the church remind us to pray for the leaders
of worship and the teachers of young persons.
When we downplay our life of faith or the joy of worship,
renew us.
When we feel we do not have to learn more, or participate in
the service of the faith community, inspire us to think again.
When we focus on ourselves and do not cherish the life of the
wider church, open our eyes to worthwhile partnership and
mission beyond our boundaries.
We are deeply privileged to be members of our church family,
and we believe we will grow as we share in its work.
*As members and friends of this church family, as
members of the family,*
**enable us to realize our responsibilities and our
opportunities.**

*We realize, O God, that in all the families of which we are
a part, we are able to rely on you.*
You will not let us stay downhearted because of temporary
setbacks and loss of self-esteem.
You will enable us to show compassion when the downhearted
look to us.
You will enable us to see our failures as a foundation for new
endeavours.
You will provide the stamina when hard decisions and hard
testing are upon us.
Your love will hold us safe, whatever befalls us, and will not
fail us when your eternal time becomes our time.
**Our membership in families will sustain us and
challenge us.**

Another Way

1. Sing the first four lines of *Would You Bless Our Homes and Families* (*Voices United* #556) after each prayer section.

2. From the gospel reading, focus on *Jesus reveals the Spirit of truth.*

Jesus reveals the Spirit of truth.
In the Spirit of truth, we will question and doubt our beliefs
    and scriptures freely.
In the Spirit of truth, we will determine how the local
    community sees us and how our faith community and
    buildings can best serve it.
In the Spirit of truth, we will steadily support our mission
    funds.
Jesus reveals the Spirit of truth.
As faithful disciples so will we!

7th Sunday of Easter

LECTIONARY READINGS

Acts 1:6–14
Psalm 68:1–10, 32–35
1 Peter 4:12–14, 5:6–11
John 17:1–11   Luke 24:44–53 – The Ascension of Jesus

*Jesus is ascended; the disciples wait for the coming
of the Holy Spirit at Pentecost.*

*Have one person mime impatient waiting by looking at his/her watch,
pacing up and down, checking a flight document, etc.*

We wait for the world to change, loving God.
We wait for understanding between Israel and the Arab nations.
We wait for the oil industry to be as concerned about spills
   and emissions as profits.
We wait for a globally organized response to natural disasters.
We wait for same gender weddings to be as accepted as the
   weddings of straight couples.
We wait but we do not wait patiently.
We will see what we can do to hasten change.

We wait for the plight of the suffering to change, loving God.
We know of persons who are kept waiting for the results of a
   job interview.
We know of patients left for hours without treatment in
   emergency departments.
We know of nursing staff members who are abused by
   patients, and of patients abused by nursing staff.
We know of children who are ignored by teachers, and of
   teachers who are treated harshly by students.
We know of conflicts within the family circle that are kept
   hidden when plain speaking or counselling is needed.
We wait but we do not wait patiently.
We will see what we can do to hasten change.

We wait for the church to change, loving God.
When will the whole range of ministries – diaconal and
   ordained, Sunday school teaching and music, cleaning and

financial – be seen as equally important?
When will the mission of church members to the local
    neighbourhood be seen as essential?
When will the leaders of all the church groups get the
    appreciation they deserve?
We wait but we do not wait patiently.
We will see what we can do to hasten change.

We wait for change within ourselves, loving God.
We realize we judge ourselves more severely than we need.
We know we sometimes judge others without having all the facts.
We believe our spiritual side needs time, encouragement, and
    learning opportunities in order to develop.
We struggle to maintain a healthy diet.
We are certain we could be more patient with those around us.
We are sure that there are leisure activities we might try out,
    and some we might give up.
We wait but we do not wait patiently.
We will see what we can do to hasten change.

Another Way

1. **Insert a time of silence at the end of the petitions.**

We wait for the world to change, loving God.
We wait for understanding between Israel and the Arab
    nations…
We wait for same gender weddings to be as accepted as the
    weddings of straight couples.
(Time of silent reflection.)
We wait but we do not wait patiently.
We will see what we can do to hasten change.

2. **Weave in the verses of the ascension hymn *Forsaking Chariots
    of Fire* (*Voices United* #192), one after each section of the
    prayer.**

SEASON AFTER PENTECOST
Pentecost Sunday

LECTIONARY READINGS
Acts 2:1–21 or Numbers 11:24–30
Psalm 104:24–34, 35b
1 Corinthians 12:3b–13 or Acts 2:1–21
John 20:19–23 or John 7:37–39

They were all filled with the Holy Spirit...and whoever calls out to the Lord for help will be saved.

Come to our world, mind and heart changing Holy Spirit!
Transform the violence we see in the groups ranged against each other in the Middle East through communication, understanding, and the will for peace.
Transform the racial labelling and prejudice we experience in our town/city through talking, working, and playing together.
Transform the gross indifference to the fate of our planet – air and water polluted, forests clear-cut, fossil fuels exhausted – through the will to conserve and live more simply.
With your unseen but effective influence,
Holy Spirit, we can do it!

Come to the places of the suffering, healing Holy Spirit!
Bring peace where industrial strife causes resentment and inconvenience.
Bring reconciliation where conflict mars the bonds of family or friendship.
Bring patient endurance where sickness restricts normal activity or ends accustomed patterns of living.
Bring hope where the ache of bereavement is felt or the loss of control is a reality.
We pray for those we know who are going through tough times *(time of silent reflection)*.
With your unseen but effective influence,
Holy Spirit, we can do it!

Come to our faith community, Holy Spirit of fellowship!
Search out and meet the obvious and the hidden needs within
    our church.
Encourage each member to give of their time, talent, and
    money for the common good.
Lift the eyes of your people to perceive the crying needs that
    lie beyond this church and this nation.
Clarify the pattern of service and the quality of commitment
    we show as those who are called Christians.
With your unseen but effective influence,
Holy Spirit, we can do it!

Come and restore each one of us, life-giving Spirit!
When we are reluctant to make the first move towards
    friendship;
when we feel overshadowed and cry out in despair;
when hurt goes on and on, and rejection is experienced;
when depression sets in and bitterness is keen;
when it seems there is no one to share our dismay or our joy;
with you as our companion, Holy Spirit, we can be
    restored!

Another Way

1. **Have two groups of people stand at the front of the church.
   The members of group one all speak English only. The
   members of group two speak other languages. Have the
   group two people say, "We are filled with the Holy Spirit" in
   their different languages, all at the same time, while group
   one says, "How wonderful! We understand! They are saying,
   'We are filled with the Holy Spirit!'"**

2. **Sing the first verse of *There's a Spirit in the Air* (*Voices United*
   #582) or the chorus of *Spirit, Open My Heart* (*More Voices* #79)
   after each section.**

3. **Use "We wait for the Spirit" as a response.**

We wait for the Spirit *(pause)*.
We wait for the Spirit to speak to our world, a world where
   despair and hunger are an ever-present reality.
We wait for the Spirit *(pause)*.
We wait for the Spirit to speak to our society, a society where
   those who have much get richer and the poor struggle.
We wait for the Spirit *(pause)*.
We wait for the Spirit to speak to the landlords of our locality
   who leave needed repairs undone.
We wait for the Spirit *(pause)*.
We wait,
and we hear the Spirit calling us to action.

Follow the same pattern for the other sections.

Trinity Sunday
First Sunday after Pentecost

LECTIONARY READINGS
Genesis 1:1—2:4a
Psalm 8
2 Corinthians 13:11–13
Matthew 28:16–20

God's authority in Jesus.

Wonderful Creator, Eternal One, the universe and all beings praise you.
Your gifts are endless, O God.
Your power is there within the mighty oceans.
Your creativity is found in the words of poems, songs, and
   sacred scriptures.
Your love is seen in the smile of child for her mother.
We will respond to you as we use creation carefully, cherish
   creativity, and hold our children precious.
God at the heart of creation,
Eternal One,
we praise you.

Eternal One, giver of Jesus, saints of past generations and Jesus-followers of today praise you.
The gifts of your chosen one are wonder-full:
the compassion of Jesus for the mentally and physically sick,
the care of Jesus for those who are bereaved,
the anger of Jesus for those who are unjustly treated.
We will respond to your gift of Jesus by speaking out and
   working against the unjust powerful ones as we help the
   sick and troubled, and as we stand beside the bereaved.
We remember our families, friends, and those in our church
   family today *(time of silent reflection)*.
God, whose supreme gift to humankind was Jesus Christ,
Eternal One,
we praise you.

Eternal One, giver of the Holy Spirit, the inspired faith communities of past generations and present-day workers in the Spirit praise you.

The gifts of the Spirit are amazing.

Persons of different racial groups worship joyfully together.

Those who seek to control are named and confronted.

The downtrodden are lifted up and the desolate comforted.

We will respond to the gift of the Spirit as we fight prejudice, stand with the poor, and comfort those who suffer loss.

God, who works, and will always work through the Spirit,

Eternal One,

we praise you.

God, giver of Creation, giver of Jesus, giver of the Holy Spirit, eternally One, we praise you.

You meet us at our point of greatest need and befriend us.

You bind us in families and communities for purpose, fellowship, and support.

You call us to your service and give us a mission.

You encourage us to hear the affirmation of friends.

You do not accept the limitations we place on ourselves.

God, loved and trusted one, in time and beyond time,

Eternal One,

we praise you.

Another Way

1. Use "and remember, I am with you always, to the end of the age" from the gospel reading as the prayer emphasis.

The spirit of Jesus is with us always.

In the spirit of Jesus, we support the powerless – those who have no job, those who need to work at two jobs to make ends meet.

The spirit of Jesus is with us always.

In the spirit of Jesus we support the dispirited – those who have been rejected by family members, those whose friends have dropped away *(time of silent reflection)*.

The spirit will never leave us,

we have nothing to fear.

The spirit of Jesus is with us always.
In the spirit of Jesus we face the trials and bleak times of life.
The spirit of Jesus is with us always.
In the spirit of Jesus, we stand beside the despised and
    forgotten – the strangers to our country, the transients, the
    mentally challenged *(time of silent reflection)*.
The spirit will never leave us,
we have nothing to fear.

Follow the same pattern for the other sections.

2. The song *Don't Be Afraid* (*More Voices* #90) could be woven
   into this prayer.

3. Sing the first verse of *Three Things I Promise* (*More Voices*
   #176) or other Trinity hymn after each prayer section.

Sunday between
May 29 & June 4 inclusive
Proper 4 [9] (if after Trinity Sunday)

LECTIONARY READINGS

Genesis 6:9–22, 7:24, 8:14–19   **or**   Deuteronomy 11:18–21,
Psalm 46   26–28
                                             Psalm 31:1–5, 19–24

Romans 1:16–17, 3:22b–28, (29–31)
Matthew 7:21–29

God our rock, our strong foundation.

God will not leave us! God will not leave our world.
Though conflict rages between nations *(give current examples)*,
though violent acts confront us in our newspaper and on the
   TV screen,
though drinking and driving is a reality in our community,
though family conflicts rage,
though newcomers to our country are exploited,
though present-day prophets are ignored,
there is a secure place, a place of hope, a place where
   reconciliation is reality and peace is found.
And God is there,
our rock, our strong foundation.

God will not leave us! God will not leave the troubled.
Though secure work is no more,
though financial foundations crumble,
though the storms of illness come unexpectedly, and caregivers are in turmoil because they cannot meet all needs,
though accidents happen, and increasing age forces a change
   in lifestyle or direction,
though death comes within the family, or to friends,
we remember our families, friends, and those in our church
   family today *(time of silent reflection)*.
There is a secure place, a place of healing and comfort, a place
   of new vision.
And God is with us there,
our rock, our strong foundation.

God will not leave us! God will not leave the faith community.

Though the church family is challenged by interest in other Sunday activities and the values of the "must buy it now" society,

though cooperation with other local faith communities comes slowly,

though it is difficult to sustain help for the powerless ones,

though it is difficult to build enthusiasm for giving to needy communities remote from our own,

there is a secure place, a place of generous sharing, a place of commitment.

And God is with us there,
our rock, our strong foundation.

Neither will God leave any one of us!

Though soulless routine holds us back,

though depression saps our strength,

though the choices we make don't work out,

though friends let us down,

though the way ahead is not clear,

though guilt clouds our happiness,

there is a secure place, a place of self-confidence, a place where we are loved.

And God is with us there,
our rock, our strong foundation.

Another Way

1. Sing one verse of verses 1–3 and 5 of *How Firm a Foundation* (*Voices United* #660) as each section is prayed. Or sing *Like A Rock* (*More Voices* #92) (with or without the actions) after each verse.

2. Ask a congregational member to construct two model houses. Place one on a sand base and fix the other securely to a piece of rock or a stone. Before the prayer is offered, hold the base and rock each house back and forth. Notice how the house on the sand moves easily, and how the house fixed to the rock remains secure.

3. Use the rock image in a fully responsive prayer.

Secure, intentions firmly set on the rock,
the just strike at *(current example)* will not founder.
Secure, intentions firmly set on the rock,
the pensioners at *(current example)* will retain their rights.
Secure, intentions firmly set on the rock,
parents will strongly oppose the closure of *(current example)*
    (the local school).
Secure, intentions firmly set on the rock,
sex trade workers will get respect and protection.
(Time of silent reflection.)
We will make sure that God's rock of justice does not move.

Secure, intentions firmly set on the rock,
we have the courage to stand up to dominant members of our
    family.
Secure, intentions firmly set on the rock,
we have the courage to say No! to an unwise course of action
    that friends would have us follow.
Secure, intentions set firmly on the rock,
we have the courage to engage a skill or talent that has
    remained hidden for so long.
We are sure that in our courageous course of action,
    God, our rock, is with us.

Follow the same pattern for the other sections.

Sunday between
June 5 & 11 inclusive
Proper 5 [10] (If after Trinity Sunday)

LECTIONARY READINGS

Genesis 12:1–9 **or** Hosea 5:15—6:6
Psalm 33:1–12 Psalm 50:7–15

Romans 4:13–25
Matthew 9:9–13, 18–26

If we have faith, the situation will change for the better.

We have faith and we trust that change is possible.
We believe that nations in conflict can be reconciled *(offer present-day examples)*.
We believe that unemployed persons will have a chance for a fulfilling job.
We believe that marginalized racial groups will find acceptance and understanding.
We believe that women will be as well accepted as engineers and heavy equipment operators as men.
We believe that the protests of those without power will be heard.
It seems hard to believe in change, O God,
but with faith everything is possible.

We have faith and we trust that change is possible.
Family members shunned because they are gay will be accepted.
Persons devastated by chronic disease will get relief.
Persons unexpectedly sick will come to terms with their problems.
Friends and family members will have insight into their treatment.
Those without family and friends will have support in hard times.
The bereaved will be given their own time to grieve *(time of silent reflection)*.
It seems hard to believe in change, O God,
but with faith everything is possible.

We have faith and we trust that change is possible.
We will see baptisms, weddings, and funerals as gateways to
the faith community.
We will be receptive to fresh ways of worship and learning.
We will welcome newcomers gently, and carefully bring them
into fellowship.
We will be ready to study injustice and act on what we learn.
We will cultivate a global sense of mission.
It seems hard to believe in change, O God,
but with faith everything is possible.

If we have faith, we trust that change is possible.
Our dependence on another will be replaced by our
determination to accept responsibility.
Our confusion around human suffering will be replaced by
practical steps to relieve suffering.
Our reluctance to move ahead will be replaced with a
readiness to venture out.
Our bringing to mind past failures will be replaced by leaving
the past in the past.
Our difficulty in seeing the relevance of our Christian faith
will be replaced with a desire to work in the spirit of Christ.
It seems hard to believe in change, O God,
but with faith everything is possible.

Another Way

1. **Use the song *Gather Us In* (*More Voices* #7) after each verse.**

2. **Focus on radical turnaround from the gospel reading:**
   Matthew the tax collector becomes a disciple of Jesus.

We will work for radical change, O God.
School board members will ensure that youngsters from racial
minorities get the specialized education they need to succeed.
Politicians from different parties will vision together to protect
the environment and conserve energy.
Employers will provide an opportunity for all workers to benefit
from the profitability of their company.
We will encourage them,
and we will work with them.

We will work for radical change, O God.
Congregations will see the need to renovate their buildings to
    meet contemporary challenges, or will be prepared to sell them.
Traditional patterns of ministry will be challenged and
    changed.
We will do nothing on our own that can be done in co-
    operation with other congregations or faith groups
The local social groups, youth groups, and businesses will be
    asked what the church can do for them.
There will be a drive to give as much for mission-supported
    groups overseas as for local needs.
We will encourage them,
and we will work with them.

Follow the same pattern for the other sections.

3. After each prayer section, have a different person say, "I
    believe change is possible in our world" "...among the
    suffering," "...in the church," "...in my own life."

Sunday between
June 12 & 18 inclusive
Proper 6 [11] (if after Trinity Sunday)

LECTIONARY READINGS

Genesis 18:1–15 (21:1–7)   **or**   Exodus 19:2–8a
Psalm 116:1–2, 12–19   Psalm 100

Romans 5:1–8
Matthew 9:35—10:8 (9–23)

The need for followers of Jesus is great.

We need people to work with the spirit of Jesus.
Then the politicians will be held accountable for the plight of
   low income families and the lack of adequate housing on
   native reserves.
Then the need for pure air and the preservation of good
   agricultural land for our grandchildren will be taken seriously.
Then a college or university education will depend on the
   ability of the student, not the ability to pay tuition fees.
Then those advanced in years will be respected, even if they
   can't control their own lives.
**We pray to God that men and women will hear the call,
and work with the spirit of Jesus.**

We need people to work with the spirit of Jesus.
Are there those who will identify the suffering and insist on
   care for them?
Are there those who will stand beside former prisoners and
   advocate with prospective employers for them?
Are there those who will listen carefully to the stories of those
   who are addicted and help them find another way and a
   higher power?
Are there those who will sit with the sick and frightened who
   have no one to share their fear?
Are there those who will listen to persons who have
   experienced a crushing loss?
We remember those we know who are suffering. As we pray,

we remember our families, friends, and those in our church family *(time of silent reflection)*.

We pray to God that men and women will hear the call, **and work with the spirit of Jesus.**

We need people to work with the spirit of Jesus.

We need persons in government and business who know what is right and will not accept shady practices.

We need present-day disciples who listen for God's call and respond, "Here I am. Send me!" They are needed to preach, to teach, and to provide pastoral care.

We need persons to care for the children and youth of our congregation. We will train them.

We need workers overseas who will teach English and bring business, water, and nursing skills in the name of God's Anointed One.

We pray to God that men and women will hear the call, **and work with the spirit of Jesus.**

And God calls us, each one of us, to work with the spirit of Jesus.

We will be motivated to discover and work out our ministries.

We will ignore the attractions of better money or benefits if the work is not faithful.

We will not fear the stigma of being thought "religious" or "pious" or too heavenly to be of any earthly use.

We will not fear the threats of the powerful, or the scorn of those who "know it all."

We will remember the caring empathetic work of Jesus and simply find our own sphere to do that work in.

It is our prayer that when we hear God's call, we will joyfully respond and work with the spirit of Jesus.

Another Way

1. After each section, have one person say, "Are you willing to work for Jesus Christ?" and another say, "Sure, what can I do?"

2. Sing one verse of *I Have Called You by Your Name* (*More Voices* #161) after each section.

3. Use a "disciple" hymn such as *In Loving Partnership* (*Voices United* #603) or the chorus of *Jesu, Jesu, Fill Us with Your Love* (*Voices United* #593) in the prayer.

4. Turn the prayer into a drama of persons called to do necessary "kingdom" work. Use biblical names but have the modern disciples called to essential contemporary tasks. Use some of the tasks alluded to in the prayer.

Christian: Peter, you are a guy with special construction skills, and you are of native ancestry. We need someone to head up a project team to renovate houses on the Falling Buffalo Reserve. Are you up to the challenge?

Peter: Well, I am pretty happy with my condo renovation work in Calgary, but sure, I am willing.

Christian: Matthew, I first met you when you were doing my tax return, but the Happy Time Seniors' Village is desperate for an accountant. Not just to keep the books but first to straighten them out. What about it?

Matthew: What?! And give up my $80,000 a year private practice?! Okay, okay, since it's you, Christian, and since they are in such a mess, I'll do it.

Sunday between
June 19 & 25 inclusive
Proper 7 [12]

LECTIONARY READINGS

Genesis 21:8–21	**or**	Jeremiah 20:7–13
Psalm 86:1–10, 16–17		Psalm 69:7–10 (11–15), 16–18

Romans 6:1b–11
Matthew 10:24–39

It is no easy job following Jesus.

Why can the nations of the world not forget their differences?

We pray for a peace that lasts between Israel and Palestine *(or current situation of conflict)*.

We pray for a peace that lasts in the divided country of Sudan *(or current area of need)*.

Why can the powerless in our community not find support?

We pray that the homeless and those without resources are able to speak out.

We pray for those who use the emergency shelters and the food banks of our town/city.

We pray for those who go the hard route of lobbying elected representatives.

We pray for those who protest without violence.

Christ stands beside the hopeless and the war-scarred innocent.

Christ stands beside those who support the powerless.

Where does our Christian approach lead us?

To be a follower of Jesus is a tough calling.

We will take the rough with the smooth.

Why can the sick and the well not be treated equally?

We pray for an equal distribution of health resources in this nation.

We pray for creative ways to diagnose and treat those in remote areas.

We pray for those in constant pain, and for the dying.
We pray for family members who constantly care for the
chronically sick.
We pray for family counsellors who hear the heartbreaking
experiences of women, men, and children and we pray for
grief counsellors who enter the empty places of those who
have lost loved ones.
Christ stands with the sick, the confused, those who have
suffered loss, and those who feel alone. And Christ stands
with those who are especially on our hearts and minds this
day *(time of silent reflection)*.
What does our Christian faith call us to do?
To be a follower of Jesus is a tough calling.
We will take the rough with the smooth.

 *Why is it so hard for the values of Jesus Christ promoted
by the church to find acceptance?*
We pray for faith community members who insist that local
congregations raise justice issues.
We pray for those who have suffered because they advocate gay
rights and sanctuary for the oppressed within the church.
We pray for those who welcome persons ignored by "polite
society" into the church.
We pray for those who promote the questioning and critical
study of Christian belief and scriptures in the local church.
We pray for those who affirm that promoting spiritual values
is a priority in a materialistic society.
We pray for those who see the local church as a small but vital
part of the Body of Christ worldwide.
To be a follower of Jesus is a tough calling.
We will take the rough with the smooth.

 Why is it so difficult to be numbered among Christ's followers?
We ask for the will to venture out when it's easier to stay close
to home.
We ask for a good friend to support us when we go against the
stream, a friend unafraid to tell it like it is.
We pray for the courage to speak the truth when it's easier to
evade the issue.
We pray for patient endurance in the face of envy and criticism.
Christ stands with those who take the uncomfortable, risky, but
faithful road.

Will our Christian discipleship lead us through difficulty and opposition to a life that satisfies spirit, heart, and mind?
To be a follower of Jesus is a tough calling.
We will take the rough with smooth.

Another Way

1. Instead of a said prayer, sing *Will You Come and Follow Me* (*Voices United* #567). At the end of each verse stop the hymn and, ask the congregation, "So what might that mean to you?"

   You could arrange with a congregant to answer what that might mean to him/her in light of the week's world events and his/her own experience. You might have her/him suggest the challenges and joys. Have another congregant answer the question after verse two. As leader, have a clear idea of the content that you would like offered. You will find that there will be an opportunity.

2. Before the prayer, the worship leader says, "There are some tough jobs: nursing on a busy ward; working on a bridge way above the ground; landing a plane in bad weather. And to be a committed Christian in these secular times, to keep the faith among people who couldn't care less, to stand up for the things Christ would stand up for in the workplace, isn't easy!"

3. Have a time of silence at the end of each section of the prayer (just before the response).

Sunday between
June 26 & July 2 inclusive
Proper 8 [13]

LECTIONARY READINGS

Genesis 22:1–14   **or**   Jeremiah 28:5–9
Psalm 13   Psalm 89:1–4, 15–18

Romans 6:12–23
Matthew 10:40–42

The people of Jesus Christ will find a welcome.

 Who in this polluted and troubled world are welcome?
God welcomes local, national, and international peacemakers.
God welcomes those who provide the means to use wind and
    solar energy.
God welcomes those who promote gardens in the cities, and those
    who share surplus grain and fruit with developing countries.
God welcomes those who do not give up on conflict resolution.
God welcomes the despised: those who clean drains and
    toilets, collect debts, or who are forced into prostitution or
    gambling work in order to survive.
In the strength of God,
we will be among those who welcome.

 Who among the suffering are welcome?
God supports those whose lack of confidence saps their ability
    to find rewarding work.
The Holy One welcomes those with physical or mental
    illnesses who can laugh and enjoy life.
The Holy One welcomes those who are downhearted and
    despondent, and those good friends who support them.
God welcomes the care-giving health bringers who see their
    job as a calling.
God welcomes those who speak out for exercise and nutritious
    food, and encourage others to healthy ways.
God gently welcomes family members and friends who
    allow the grieving ones to express their anger and feel the
    emptiness.

We join with the Holy One in welcoming them now, and
hold up the sick and sorrowing before God *(time of silent
reflection)*.

God's welcoming acceptance is with those going through
conflict and tough times at work, and those bullied or picked
on at school.

In the strength of God,
we will be among those who welcome.

Who in the faith community are welcome?

God welcomes those who say very little but quietly help
people who are in trouble.

God welcomes those who call on faith community members to
risk, venture, and enliven the church.

God welcomes those who question – the doubters, and the
seekers after spiritual truth.

God welcomes the newcomer and the stranger from near at
hand and far away.

And God welcomes into the faith community those who have
nowhere else to go.

In the strength of God,
we will be among those who welcome.

Wonderfully, amazingly, God welcomes us!

As those who are anxious to use skills, gifts, and talents to
bring God's kingdom closer,
God welcomes us.

As those who are painfully aware of our faults and failings,
God welcomes us, and reminds us of our many good gifts.

As those who find it hard to overcome apathy and despondency,
God welcomes us and gives us confidence to begin anew.

As those with relationships, God rejoices in companionship
and intimacy and calls us to seek out the lonely.

**We are royally welcomed by the Holy One. We extend
that welcome to those who feel rejected and unloved.**

Another Way

1. Sing one verse of *Welcome, Jesus, You Are Welcome* (*More
   Voices* #137) after each section.

2. Whoever gives a cup of cold water to one of these little ones... (Matthew 10:42)

Have eight glasses of water on the Communion table. Have individual congregational members primed to role play.

Fred: *(dressed in dirty plumber's coveralls)* Sorry I smell so strong! I've just been cleaning a drain.
Leader: Someone's got to do the job. Here's a cup of water. And welcome!

April: *(looking like death warmed up)* I don't know how I am going to get through the day. I feel so miserable and depressed.
Leader: It's not like you, April, but – well – maybe we could talk about it after the service. And you are welcome however you feel, and here is a cup of water to refresh you.

Follow the same pattern for the other sections.

3. Have congregants welcome each other in different ways: one pair shakes hands, another hugs warmly, a third exchange kisses on the cheek. Then have the whole congregation stand and welcome each other.

Sunday between
July 3 & 9 inclusive
Proper 9 [14]

LECTIONARY READINGS

Genesis 24:34–38, 42–49, 58–67   **or**   Zechariah 9:9–12
Psalm 45:10–17   Psalm 145:8–14
or Song of Solomon 2:8–13

Romans 7:15–25a
Matthew 11:16–19, 25–30

Those who find and follow the way of Jesus Christ find peace.

We seek your Peace, O God.
The peace the poet of the 23rd Psalm found in his time
    of grief.
The peace that Ruth found in faithfully following Rachel.
The peace that Mary found in accepting the coming of
    your Chosen One.
The active peace that Jesus brought through working to
    counter injustice and selfishness.
Your peace, O God.

Peace for our world.
Fear is present in the violent and troubled world that is ours,
    O God.
The headlines in the newspapers tell of car bombs and the
    deaths of soldiers in *(use current examples, as applicable)*.
The television news speaks of a child who is missing, and
    another program tells of the millions of children who are at
    risk of abuse and injury through dangerous work.
This week I saw an angry encounter on the main street of our
    town.
These events make us afraid.
What we seek, oh most caring God, is peace: a peace that
    penetrates to the root of our fear; a peace that renders fear
    impotent, harmless, and irrelevant.
Your peace, O God.
The peace that goes beyond all human understanding.

Peace among those who are suffering.
Fear is a reality among those who are sick and depressed,
among those whose well of creativity has dried up,
among those who put off today's work until tomorrow,
among those who have covered up their own addiction, or the
    addiction of a friend or colleague, because they were afraid
    of the consequences,
among those in one of the caring professions who are
    overworked but refuse to take a break,
among those who have been afraid to face their symptoms for
    a long time,
among those diagnosed or being treated for one of the cancers,
    among those who mourn the loss of a loved one long after her
    death, and are afraid to accept that their grieving is not yet over
    (silent time of remembering and reflection).
What we seek for all, most caring God, is peace: a peace
    that penetrates to the root of fear, a peace that renders fear
    impotent, harmless, and irrelevant.
Your peace, O God.
The peace that goes beyond all human understanding.

Peace in the church.
Fear is a reality among those who worry about the loss of
    Christian influence and the decline in the number of
    Christian services for weddings, funerals, and baptisms.
Fear is present when it seems that secular societal values
    steadily encroach on the life of the church.
Fear is present when modern technology and music forms are
    proposed, such as *(an upfront band, or PowerPoint).*
Fear is present when commitment to church membership is
    seen as unusual and unnecessary.
What we seek, O most caring God, is peace in our faith community:
    a peace that penetrates to the root of our fear, a peace that
    renders fear impotent, harmless, and irrelevant.
Your peace, O God.
The peace that goes beyond all human understanding.

Peace within each one of us.
We know the lack of peace is an ever-present reality.
We worry about the conflicts that disturb relationships.
We worry about the lives of those close to us – our children,
    grandchildren, parents, and friends.

We worry about our work and leisure activities, and especially about what people think of us.

We worry about our life's direction, and our inability to reach our goals and live our dreams.

What we seek is your peace, O God.

For we know if we feel, accept, and work for your peace, then nothing in the world around us will create fear anymore.

Another Way

1. Sing one of the many songs of peace (such as *Make Me a Channel of Your Peace, Voices United* #684) before, during, or after the prayer or prayer section.

2. Use the word *peace* as a mantra throughout the prayer.

Peace, peace, peace.
In our troubled world *(news item),*
we pray for peace. *(Time of silent reflection.)*
Peace, peace, peace.
In our town/city there is uncertainty *(news item).*
We pray for peace. *(Time of silent reflection.)*
Living God,
make us channels of your peace.

Follow the same pattern for the other sections.

Sunday between
July 10 & 16 inclusive
Proper 10 [15]

LECTIONARY READINGS

Genesis 25:19–34   **or**   Isaiah 55:10–13
Psalm 119:105–112   Psalm 65:(1–8) 9–13

Romans 8:1–11
Matthew 13:1–9, 18–23

> *Jesus said, "A sower went out to sow, and as he sowed some
> seeds fell on the path and others fell on rocky ground."*

The continuing distrust between Israelis and Palestinians *(or
current example)*, the peace process at a standstill.
Stony ground.
The effects of the extremes of climate – floods, forest fires,
scorching heat.
Stony ground.
Disagreement between medical groups and government about
funds for research.
Stony ground.
Loving God, may concern for future generations, efforts to
bring help to those in tough situations, and an openness to
other points of view, bring an abundant harvest.

Illnesses which do not yield to treatment and long treatment
waiting lists.
Stony ground.
Troubled relationships for which there seems no possibility
for resolution or change.
Stony ground.
The barren, empty place of bereavement *(time of silent
remembering and reflection)*.
Stony ground.
Loving God, may a move to wholeness and healing bring a
harvest of peace.
May the desire to begin again bring a harvest of reconciliation.
May the gentle comfort of friends bring a harvest of hope.

A faith life that is stale and unrewarding.
Stony ground.
Apathy, and a "leave it to someone else" attitude in the church.
Stony ground.
An unwillingness to cooperate with wider church groups, or
dialogue with other faith groups.
Stony ground.
May a renewal of spiritual practice, a willingness to take
responsibility, and a reaching out to neighbours in Christ
and as friends in the Spirit, bring a harvest of religious
relevance and faithful action.

The feeling of being stuck in circumstances that cannot be
changed.
Stony ground.
Fears hidden deep within us that cannot be released.
Stony ground.
An inability to express strongly held opinions because of what
others might think.
Stony ground.
Loving God, may renewed determination bring a harvest of
new opportunities.
May a willingness to express our fears to another bring a
harvest of freedom.
May the courage to stand for what is just and right bring a
harvest of confidence and action.
God of the good seed be praised!

Another Way

1. Sing one verse of *Through the Heart of Every City* (*Voices
   United* #584) after each section, repeating verse one after the
   last verse.

2. Spread a bucketful of stones onto a piece of cloth on the floor
   at the front of the sanctuary. During the prayer, have a person
   pick up one stone at a time and drop it noisily into the metal
   bucket.

3. Focus on the word as the seed.

We hear many superficial words, O God, but they are not your word.

We are told that if we just read the Bible we will find God speaking to us. But we are called to read carefully and with faithful intelligence.

We are told that if we open the church doors the seekers will walk through and participate in our worship and programs. But we are called to listen to those who are outside the faith community and to respond to what they need.

We hear many superficial words, O God, but they are not your word.

We are told to forget our anxieties and put our troubled feelings behind us, but we are called to find a trusted one to share our feelings with, someone who will stay with us in life's storms.

We are told to keep a low profile over our concern for a local issue and not to rock the boat, but we are called to advocate for what is just.

We are called to make our presence felt.

Follow the same pattern for the other sections.

Sunday between
July 17 & 23 inclusive
Proper 11 [16]

LECTIONARY READINGS

Genesis 28:10–19a   **or**   Wisdom of Solomon 12:13,
Psalm 139:1–12, 23–24   16–19 or
                                     Isaiah 44:6–8
                                     Psalm 86:11–17

Romans 8:12–25
Matthew 13:24–30, 36–43

God's faithful ones sow the good seed.

In our world there are those who sow the good seed.
They sow the seeds of practical help for those who do not
   know where the next meal is coming from.
They give seed loans to those who are starting off in business,
   and money to people whom the banks won't talk to.
They sow seeds of hope for parents trying to balance the
   challenges of home life, work, their social lives, and
   activities for their children.
They sow seeds of peace for persons confronting each other
   in local government and national leaders in conflict *(time of
   silent reflection)*.
We support those who sow the good seed.
God is with them, and God is with us.
With joy we await the harvest.

Among the troubled there are those who sow the good seed.
Social workers bring understanding to those going through the
   storms of life.
Child care workers bring relief to parents and calm to
   disturbed children.
Sensitive family doctors get the confidence of their troubled
   patients.
Ministers, counsellors and funeral directors bring peace and a
   new reality to those who mourn.

We remember those who are sick, troubled, and those who are
    bereaved *(time of silent reflection)*.
We support those who sow the good seed.
God is with them, and God is with us.
With joy we await the harvest.

Within the church there are those who sow the good seed.
We give thanks for clergy and lay leaders who preach, teach,
    and offer pastoral care to the downhearted.
We give thanks to those who encourage and challenge children
    and youth to serve others and to have confidence in their
    own abilities.
We give thanks for those who advocate for the powerless.
We give thanks to those who call us to look beyond our
    local faith community to the needs of those in distant and
    developing countries.
We support those who sow the good seed.
God is with them, and God is with us.
With joy we await the harvest.

We know that we have the responsibility of sowing good seed.
We have the chance to inspire and challenge those around us.
Our family members need a listening ear, and our friends need
    us to build them up.
Our social groups look to us for support, and to do the jobs no
    one else wants to do.
We know if we walk or exercise regularly others will follow
    our example.
Our faith community relies on us to worship and give
    regularly and take an active part in the life of the church.
And there are other areas where we are called to sow the good
    seed *(time of silent reflection)*.
God is with us as we work as God's seed sowers; there
will be a joyful harvest!

Another Way

1. Focus on sowing seeds.

God's seed sowers
are active in the peace movement,
are with the initiators of *(group for change in the community)*,
seek accessible facilities for the challenged ones in this
    community,
give generously when natural disasters strike.
Show us the need for seeds, O God.
We want to sow.

God's seed sowers
are in on the ground floor to raise money for new hospital
    equipment *(local examples)*,
are among the first to volunteer for *(meals on wheels) (local
    examples)*,
give practical help to families that have a family member who
    is sick,
go right over to offer support when a loved one has died.
Show us the need for seeds, O God.
We want to sow.

2. Have a short discussion about seeds that grow well in your area
and those that do not. What seed is good seed for...? Or talk
about seed money for enterprises that create work or grow
faith.

3. Use verse one of *Your Work, O God, Needs Many Hands*
(*Voices United* #537) after each prayer section.

Sunday between
July 24 & 30 inclusive
Proper 12 [17]

LECTIONARY READINGS

Genesis 29:15–28 **or** 1 Kings 3:5–12
Psalm 105:1–11, 45b Psalm 119:129–136
or Psalm 128

Romans 8:26–39
Matthew 13:31–33, 44–52

*The kingdom of heaven is a treasure and we are
called to search for it.*

***The kingdom is a treasure – God's treasure. We will search
for it in our world.***

Where there is reconciliation among enemies *(current
example)*, the treasure is found.

In a situation *(like the earthquake in Haiti or Chile or Tibet)*
where the "have" nations give money and practical support
to those who have very little, the treasure is found.

In prisons where the inmates are seen less as persons to be
punished and more as humans who have potential for good,
the treasure is found.

In schools where talented students actively support the
struggling ones, the treasure is found.

Among social workers who go the extra mile for their clients,
the treasure is found.

Count us among those, O God,
who search carefully and persistently for the kingdom.

***The kingdom is a treasure – God's treasure. We will search
for it among those most at a loss.***

The treasure is found where those who live hectically take the
time they need to read a good book or creatively work in the
garden.

The treasure is found among those who lovingly look after
elderly dependants or challenged young persons. The
treasure is found where advisors and counsellors work

tirelessly to enable persons to find jobs that meet their skills and abilities.

The treasure is found when the sick person is treated holistically, not just for the physical symptoms.

The treasure is found among persons who stay beside those who feel the loss of a loved one acutely *(time of silent reflection)*.

Count us among those, O God,
who search carefully and persistently for the kingdom.

The kingdom is a treasure – God's treasure. We will search for it within the faith community.

In a community where a newcomer feels at home and each child is nurtured, the treasure is found.

Where the church consistently dialogues with the local community and is open to its needs, the treasure is found.

Where local churches work together and search out ways of serving those most vulnerable in the area, the treasure is found.

Where overseas mission needs are held up as being as important as local needs, the treasure is found.

We are members of the faith community.
Count us among those, O God,
who search carefully and persistently for the kingdom.

The kingdom is a treasure – God's treasure. We will search for it in our everyday moments.

We will find treasure in a breathless early morning beside the lake.

We will find treasure as we experience the love and friendship of those close to us.

We will find treasure as we give our valued gifts away.

We will find treasure as we become aware of the unrealized gifts of those we meet and give them confidence to use those gifts.

We will find in our spiritual life God's treasure beyond price.

Count us among those, O God,
who search carefully and persistently for the kingdom.

Another Way

1. Sing the first verse of *Seek Ye First the Kingdom* (*Voices United* #356) after each section. Verse one of *The Kingdom of God* (*More Voices* #146), or other kingdom song could also be used in this way.

2. Dialogue with the congregation on what they consider to be "treasure" before each section of the prayer. Have in mind the tangible objects and events which you see as kingdom treasure. The prayer phrases will help you with this.

3. Hide some "treasure" at the front of the church and have a few volunteers hunt for it. There will be searching and then joy when the coins, candies, or fortune cookies are found. Make the connection between these so-called treasures and God's treasure (as in the prayer phrases above).

Sunday between
July 31 & August 6 inclusive
Proper 13 [18]

LECTIONARY READINGS

Genesis 32:22–31   **or**   Isaiah 55:1–5
Psalm 17:1–7, 15   Psalm 145:8–9, 14–21

Romans 9:1–5
Matthew 14:13–21

A miracle of compassion and sharing.

If only everyone in our world shared compassionately,
* as Jesus did,*
the refugee and the immigrant would be treated carefully,
no child would go without food or shelter or basic education,
the mentally challenged would not be thrown in jail,
women would not be afraid to name their abusers,
the powerful leaders would listen to the crying needs of those
  most vulnerable and afraid.
Jesus listened compassionately, and no one went away
* unsatisfied.*
We, too, will listen with compassion.

If only the needs of those who suffer were heard,
bullying would be dealt with quickly,
the minimum wage would be raised,
affordable housing would be made a priority,
no physically challenged person would be prevented from
  entering a washroom, a store or a hotel,
the undiagnosed would get urgent treatment, and the bereaved
  would be comforted patiently.
We remember those who are ill and those who have lost loved
  ones *(time of silent reflection).*
Jesus listened compassionately, and no one went away
* unsatisfied.*
We, too, will listen with compassion.

If only members of the faith community would listen and share,

the Bible would be read among friends and questioners, and the Gospel story would be seen as contemporary and relevant;

the history of the church would be studied and seen in a present-day context;

church buildings would be less important than the gathered people;

the call for mission to the neighbourhood would meet with a ready response;

we would hear clearly the needs of those in other lands, and respond.

Jesus listened compassionately, and no one went away unsatisfied.

We, too, will listen with compassion.

 If only we would listen and share.

If we listened we would hear the insistent whispers for help.

If we listened we would be aware of the needs right in front of us.

If we listened we would give family and friends the time they need.

If we listened – listened deeply, listened carefully, listened patiently, listened empathetically – we would hear God's word for us, take it to heart, and act on it.

Jesus listened compassionately, and no one went away unsatisfied.

We, too, will listen with compassion.

Another Way

1. **Have two persons sit facing each other on chairs at the front of the church, one miming intent listening, the other miming passionate speaking.**

2. **Have a time of reflection after each prayer section.**

3. **Dramatize a phrase from each section.**

    For example, the phrase in the church section: *The call for mission to the neighbourhood would meet with a ready response.*

Christine: I would like to see us going out to tell people in *(name of town/city)* what we are doing here at St. Andrew's. Maybe two by two, like the disciples did in the Bible.

Jim: Sounds too much like evangelizing to me. I think we would get a lot of doors shut in our faces.

Christine: Well, the locals are not rushing through our doors as it is, and we have a good worship service and fine youth activities. Why not tell people around us about it?

Jim: Well *(pause)* perhaps *(pause)*. I would need some training before I went out.

Christine: And we would make sure you get it!

Sunday between
August 7 & 13 inclusive
Proper 14 [19]

LECTIONARY READINGS

Genesis 37:1–4, 12–28   **or**   1 Kings 19:9–18
Psalm 105:1–6, 6–22, 45b   Psalm 85:8–13

Romans 10:5–15
Matthew 14:22–33

Jesus goes to the hills to pray.

A Summer Prayer of Refreshment

We praise you for this wonderful world, Creator God.
The glory of a summer morning, the sunlit fields, the rolling hills,
  and the mirror-imaged lake tell of your creative genius.
The smile of a young mother for her inquisitive laughing child
  speaks of your love for humankind.
The thoughtful, "Do you remember…?" conversation shared
  between two elderly persons reminds us of your wisdom
  communicated down the generations.
We see pictures of polluted waterways, despairing parents, and
  abused older persons,
but you have shown us, O God,
how it could be.

We praise you for your way of compassion, Loving God.
The uproarious birthday party in a group home speaks of
  · Jesus' acceptance of the mentally sick.
The careful, friendly treatment given to a stray dog in a
  shelter reflects the concern of St. Francis and the Buddha
  for all created beings.
The casserole offered with a hug to a neighbour who has lost
  their spouse reminds us of the attention that Jesus paid to
  those bereaved.
And we remember now those who are suffering and those
  who help and support them *(time of silent reflection).*
We hear tell of the rejection of mentally challenged persons, of
  pets that are neglected, and bereaved persons told to get over it,

but you have shown us, O God,
how it could be.

We thank you for Spirit alive in the church, Holy God.
The service of worship that throbs with musical joy and
    sacred silence,
the unexpected volunteer for an important task in the faith
    community,
the unforeseen sense of unity that happens when two
    churches meet to study together,
the personal testimony that makes clear the reality of faith.
We hear of the decline of the church, the neglect of spiritual
    practice, and the absence of young persons in churches,
but you have shown us, O God,
how it could be.

We thank you for your goodness to each one of us, O God.
We have friends and family members, children and
    grandchildren, nieces and nephews, who delight us.
We have hobbies, interests, and activities that excite us.
We have a faith community that is our loving church home.
We have a place in this world that is good to live in.
We are challenged by sickness, by the jobs we do, by our
    financial situations, and by some of our relationships,
**but we realize, O God, how much we have to be thankful
for.**

Another Way

1. Sing verse one of *In You There Is a Refuge* (*More Voices* #84)
   or *Father Hear the Prayer We Offer*, or *Lord, Listen to Your
   Children Praying* (*Voices United* #400) after each section.

2. At the end of the prayer, invite congregants to turn to one
   other person and tell them of one or more things for which
   they are thankful. What were they thinking about as this
   prayer was offered?

3. Allow time in each section of the prayer for congregants to add their thanksgivings either silently or (preferably) out loud.

 We thank you for your goodness to each one of us, O God.
We have friends and family members, children and grandchildren, who delight us.
We have pastimes and activities that excite us.
We have a faith community that is a church home for us.
We have a place in the world that is good to live in.
Invite congregants to offer their personal thanksgivings.
We are challenged by sickness, by the jobs we do, by our financial situations, and by some of our relationships,
but we realize, O God, how much we have to be thankful for.

Follow the same pattern for the other sections.

Sunday between
August 14 & 20 inclusive
Proper 15 [20]

LECTIONARY READINGS

Genesis 45:1–15	**or**	Isaiah 56:1, 6–8
Psalm 133		Psalm 67

Romans 11:1–2a, 29–32
Matthew 15:(10–20), 21–28

> *The conventional attitudes and complacency
> of Jesus are challenged.*

You challenge us, Living God.
You challenge us to understand the world around us, to make
sense of *(current international struggle/conflict)*.
You challenge us to understand the significance of local events,
to find the values at the core of *(local athletic/cultural/health
promotion event)*.
You challenge us to understand our neighbourhood, to understand
the needs of those who lack food and a support system.
Living God,
you challenge us, and we ask,
"How will I respond to the challenge?"

You challenge us, Living God.
You challenge us to understand the needs of the suffering.
As we recall the unmet needs of those who are struggling with
their education, those who have learning disabilities, those
able persons who lack tuition fees, we feel your challenge to
speak out for them.
As we think of family members, church family members, and
friends who are in hospital, and those who are under the
dark cloud of depression, we feel your challenge and search
for a response. In silence, we bring them to mind *(time of
silent reflection)*.
And you challenge us to remember those who have been
bereaved: those for whom loss is new and raw, and those for
whom the nagging emptiness of bereavement continues to be

felt. In silence, we bring those we know to mind and we bring to mind those who stand with them *(time of silent reflection)*.
Compassionate God,
you challenge us, and we ask,
"How will I respond to the challenge?"

You challenge us, Living God.
You challenge us to consider the essential strength of our Christian values and beliefs.
You challenge us to consider the meaning of our church membership.
We pray for *(clergy name and board chair name)* and those who share the leadership of this church as they search for Christian relevance and appropriate mission in an essentially non-Christian society.
You challenge us to support those in the wider church *(names and titles)*.
And we are aware of the challenges faced by the mission fund in its work caring for those whose names and backgrounds we will never know.
God of the church,
you challenge us, and we ask,
"How will I respond to the challenge?"

And you challenge each one of us, Living God.
You challenge us to express the joy that bubbles up from within us.
You challenge us to express the anger we keep below the surface.
You challenge us to face the doubts we have about our self-worth.
You challenge us to be open to new friendships.
You challenge us to use the talents that we know are hidden deep within us.
You challenge us to deal with guilt that disturbs us and holds us back.
You challenge us to be upfront about the reluctance to change that dulls our relationships.
Loving, personal God,
you challenge us, and we ask,
"How will I respond to the challenge?"

Another Way

1. Weave a prayer of challenge in with the prayer. Sing one verse of *Be Thou My Vision* (*Voices United* #642) or *One More Step Along the World I Go* (*Voices United* #639) or the first verse of *Guide Me, O Thou Great Jehovah* (*Voices United* #651) after each section.

2. As the Canaanite woman shows the quality of persistence, work out that theme in the prayer.

Persist!
When a friend tells you to be satisfied with your routine work,
Persist!
When the physiotherapist says you won't run again,
Persist!
When you are discouraged from seeking a second opinion,
Persist!
When a neighbour says that your time of grieving should be over,
Persist!
We think of those who today are sick or bereaved and need courage to stay the course *(time of silent reflection)*.
For them we have one strong word.
Persist!

3. Have one congregational member speak of her/his current challenges and what she/he is doing about them (work, an elderly parent, sick pet, etc.).

Sunday between
August 21 & 27 inclusive
Proper 16 [21]

LECTIONARY READINGS

| Exodus 1:8—2:10 | **or** | Isaiah 51:1–6 |
| Psalm 124 | | Psalm 138 |

Romans 12:1–8
Matthew 16:13–20

> *Jesus says, "Peter you are a rock, and on this rock
> foundation I will build my church."*

In our world we need rock solid foundations:
organizations such as the United Nations that bring nations
    together, and care for refugees and the most vulnerable;
advocacy groups such as Amnesty International that will not
    let those without a voice be forgotten;
local groups that support the poorest and most at risk –
    transients, addicts, and sex trade workers;
parents who are aware of the challenges in the school system
    and who work together to have those challenges met.
You make clear, O God,
the rock solid foundations.

***In our caring for the suffering, we need rock solid
    foundations:***
lawyers who carefully arbitrate and help those going through
    divorce or separation;
those devoted to the training of health professionals for whom
    second best is not good enough;
dentists who tell their patients, "Call me directly if you
    experience any more pain";
family practitioners who order all the necessary tests and refer
    promptly to specialists;
grief and family counsellors who take all the time that is
    necessary with their clients.
We remember those in our church and in our families who are
    going through testing times *(time of silent reflection).*

In sickness and in bereavement, we remember that those who
are suffering need reliable, compassionate, and wise persons
to be their "rocks" *(time of silent reflection)*.
You make clear, O God,
the rock solid foundations.

In our church we need rock solid foundations:
those who can be relied on to offer leadership when leadership
is in short supply;
persons who listen with their whole being when someone
from the faith community is in trouble;
persons who advocate for the wider church when it seems
that the local congregation has enough demands of its own
on talent and gifts;
those who know and respect the traditions of the church yet
are not afraid of change.
When the faith community is tested and lacks vision, the
rocks are relied on and will come through.
You make clear, O God,
the rock solid foundations.

We need rock solid foundations on which to build our own
lives:
the teaching and knowledge which trusted ones have passed
along to us;
the confidence to believe that if we need information or help
we can find it;
a set of values and beliefs arrived at through trial and error
over the years;
the support of loved ones and good friends that can be
counted on;
the certainty that God has gifted us and wants us to use all
our gifts;
the knowledge that in time and beyond time God embraces us
with love.
For now, for ever,
you make clear, O God,
the rock solid foundations.

Another Way

1. Put a large and solid rock on the Communion table, or have a builder or educator talk about the importance of good foundations.

2. Sing *How Firm a Foundation* (*Voices United* #660), verses 1–3 and 5, with one verse sung after each section is prayed, or sing *Like a Rock* (*More Voices* #92), with or without the actions, after each section.

3. You might talk with the congregation about foundation values before the prayer.

 Foundation values. You call us, O God, to express our foundation values.
We will leave the earth good for our children and grandchildren.
No child, in any country, will go to bed hungry or without safe shelter.
Education will be a right for every child and for the adult who chooses to train for another occupation.
(Time for reflection or discussion.)

 Foundation values. You call us, O God, to express our foundation values.
No adult will be passed over for a job because of his/her skin colour or facial features.
No child will be subject to bullying or being looked down on in school.
Every person will be able to access the appropriate level of care for a physical or mental health problem.
No person will denied the time they need to recover from childbirth or the death of a loved one.
(Time for reflection or discussion.)

Sunday between
August 28 & September 3 inclusive
Proper 17 [22]

LECTIONARY READINGS

Exodus 3:1–15   **or**   Jeremiah 15:15–21
Psalm 105:1–6, 23–26, 45c   Psalm 26:1–8

Romans 12:9–21
Matthew 16:21–28

Jesus speaks about his suffering and death.

The determination to act faithfully comes with a high cost.
As those around Martin Luther King found out, prejudice and
   hatred will not be deflected.
As the friends of Oscar Romero found out, the preaching of
   the powerful ones does not include "freedom for the poor."
As refugees the world over have discovered, those engaged in
   warfare have no regard for the civilians in their path.
As local government officials and those who whistle-blow on
   corporations have found, exposing authority figures may
   cost them their job.
In our own sphere of action and influence,
we have faithful choices to make.
May we give and not count the cost.

The determination to act faithfully comes with a high cost.
Those who stand up against large corporations know this.
Those who have protested against government immigration
   policies know this.
Those who have been lost among forms, bureaucrats, and
   voice mail know this.
Those who have been in dispute with health professionals
   know this.
Those who try to make clear their feelings while lying weak in
   a hospital bed know this.
Those whose voice has not been heard at the time of personal
   loss know this.
The determination to act faithfully comes with a high cost.

We pray for those who are suffering at this time, especially those
who feel they are not in control *(time of silent reflection)*.
We pray for those who have lost loved ones *(time of silent
reflection)*.
In our own sphere of action and influence,
we have faithful choices to make.
May we give and not count the cost.

 The determination to act faithfully comes with a high cost.
Clergy whose principles are at odds with the faith community
they serve are aware of this.
Faith community members whose principles are at odds with
the serving clergyperson are aware of this.
Church leaders and members who take a stand in the local
community against a low minimum wage, the exploitation
of immigrant workers, or *(insert example)* are aware of this.
The issues of global warming, same gender marriages, and the
manufacture and use of armaments, have pitted the national
church against the government, and there has been a price
to pay for their faithfulness to gospel principles.
And in our own sphere of action and influence,
we have faithful choices to make.
May we give and not count the cost.

 The determination to act faithfully comes with a high cost.
We find ourselves taking a stand against popular but costly
government policies.
We find ourselves speaking out against racially prejudiced
jokes and remarks.
We find ourselves not being able to go along with unethical
practices at work.
We find ourselves at odds with family members whose value
system is very different from our own.
We find ourselves shunned by those who play by self-serving rules.
We find ourselves in dispute with those we count as friends.
Especially in our own sphere of action and influence,
we have faithful choices to make.
May we give and not count the cost.

Another Way

1. **Before the prayer, have someone read (or say together) the first part of the Prayer of St. Francis. Read the second part after the prayer is complete.**

Lord, make me an instrument of your peace.
  Where there is hatred, let me sow love;
  where there is injury, pardon;
  where there is doubt, faith;
  where there is despair, hope;
  where there is darkness, light;
  and where there is sadness, joy.

O Divine Lover, grant that I may not so much seek
  to be consoled as to console;
  to be understood as to understand;
  to be loved as to love.
  For it is in giving that we receive;
  it is in pardoning that we are pardoned;
  and it is in dying that we are born to eternal life. Amen.

2. *If any want to become my followers, let them deny themselves and take up their cross and follow me.* Matthew 16:24

    Have a large cross at the front of the sanctuary. Have one person lift the cross as the worship leader says, "We take up the cross."

We take up the cross.
  We take up the cross in solidarity with civilians who suffer in
    time of war.
  We take up the cross in solidarity with political prisoners who
    are forgotten in their own country.
  We take up the cross in solidarity with teachers who oppose
    an increase in classroom size.
  We take up the cross in solidarity *(local issue).*
  As we know well,
    the cross is a heavy burden to carry.

We take up the cross.
We will make sure the voices of children are heard and heeded
in church.
We will make sure that our music in worship is balanced
between contemporary forms and the well-loved old favourites.
We will make sure that we invite the despised and rejected of
our local community to use our building.
As we know well,
the cross is a heavy burden to carry.

Follow the same pattern for the other sections.

Sunday between
September 4 & 10 inclusive
Proper 18 [23]

LECTIONARY READINGS

Exodus 12:1–24   **or**   Ezekiel 33:7–11
Psalm 149   Psalm 119:33–40

Romans 13:8–14
Matthew 18:15–20

*For where two or three are gathered in my name,
I am among them.*

A prayer for the ending of summer and the beginning of the new church year.

God of endings and beginnings, we come before you.
We need fresh starts in our world.
We pray for a peaceful end to the conflict in Afghanistan *(or recent example)* and the beginning of a lasting peace between Israel and Palestine.
We pray for the beginning of an organization for world peace that is effective, and
we pray for an end to hostilities that cause persons to flee their homelands as refugees.
We pray for the establishment of a global charter that enables each child to have nutritious food, education, and safety from exploitation and sexual abuse.
Just and loving God,
with you new beginnings come to life and work out purposefully.

God of endings and beginnings, we come before you.
We need fresh starts among the suffering.
We pray for the beginning of practice patterns within the health care network that enable all to have access to the best diagnostic facilities, and we pray for an end to the fear that prevents persons from seeking timely medical help.

We pray for understanding when memory loss has distorted the normal pattern of living.

We pray for a positive attitude towards those who are mentally ill and those who care for them, and an end to the prejudice that results in inferior care.

We pray for an end to the emptiness and desolation that comes with grieving, and the beginning of life that is again enjoyable, through the support of good friends and counsellors.

We pray for members of our family and our church family who are going through troubled times *(time of silent reflection)*.

Just and loving God,
with you new beginnings come to life and work out purposefully.

God of endings and beginnings, we come before you.
We need fresh starts within the church.

At this end to the summer life of the church, we give thanks for those who brought worship and fun and support to so many within the faith community *(name persons and activities)* and we pray for this faith community at the start of a new church year.

We especially bring before you, Gracious God, *(name church school teachers and helpers, those responsible for worship, music, social, and outreach activities)*.

We pray for those who are in the wider bodies/courts/ groupings of the church, that new directions that revitalize and strengthen our well-loved denomination will emerge, and that there will be an end to talk that does not result in action.

We pray for an end to seeing the mission funds as second best to local giving, and we pray for the beginning of a practical empathy for those whose needs are great but whose names we will never know.

Just and loving God,
with you new beginnings come to life and work out purposefully.

And we are aware of our personal need for fresh starts.
As we remember the personal conflicts that seem never ending, we pray for the beginning of fresh understanding and a new direction.

As we seek to bring to an end a troubled occupation or
unsatisfying leisure time activity, so we pray for energy and
enthusiasm to start those ventures that fulfill us.

We pray for an end to the fears and memories of events long
past that haunt and depress us, and the beginning of feeling
joy and excitement in the everyday moments of life.

**Gracious and ever loving God, in our endings and in our
beginnings we look only for your purpose and for the
will to fulfill your purpose. Amen.**

Another Way

1. Use symbols of endings and new beginnings in the prayer.

 This pair of sunglasses reminds me of enjoyable days on the
beach.

**We thank you, Creator God, for the glorious days of
summer.**

These autumn leaves remind me of the wonderful fall that lies
ahead.

We praise you, Creator God of all the seasons.

These comic books remind me of the easy summer reading;
these text books remind me of the study that is ahead.

Thank you, God, for "good reads" and new knowledge.

You, God, are with us in our endings and our beginnings.

 This pair of runners reminds me of healthy walks and runs in
the open air.

**These skates remind me of the winter sports that start
soon.**

This cast or bandage reminds me of an injury that happened a
few weeks ago.

**This wheelchair is a symbol of those who will have to
endure treatment in the coming months.**

We remember them, we think of them *(time of silent reflection)*.

**This empty chair reminds me of those who have lost
loved ones or suffered other losses over the summer.**

We remember them, we think of them *(time of silent reflection)*.

You, God, are with us in our endings and our beginnings.

These drawings remind us of the summer Sunday program.

This *Seasons of the Spirit* book reminds us of all the fun and interesting activities that are ahead.

This Bible reminds us of all the readings and stories we have heard over the summer.

The same Bible will be a guide and inspiration in the coming months.

These church members have led our worship in the past months.

Our minister and these church members will be our leaders as a new church year begins.

You, God, are with us in our endings and our beginnings.

2. Sing the chorus of *Grateful* (*More Voices* #182) between each prayer section.

3. Talk about this Sunday being one of a fresh start in the faith community, and how God gives us opportunities to put old ways behind us. Widen this to more general issues about fresh starts.

Sunday between
September 11 & 17 inclusive
Proper 19 [24]

LECTIONARY READINGS

Exodus 14:19–31	**or**	Genesis 50:15–21
Psalm 114 or		Psalm 103:(1–7), 8–13
Exodus 15:1b–11, 20–21		

Romans 14:1–12
Matthew 18:21–35

It is hard to forgive.

We are called on to forgive many in our world.

We want to forgive those who have resorted to violence and warfare to solve problems. We want to forgive those who have oppressed women and children.

We want to forgive those who have looked down on persons of another race or colour.

We want to forgive those who have stolen from the infirm, the gullible, and the innocent.

We are resolved to help bring change. We are resolved to support the process of change.

Peter asks Jesus, "How often should I forgive, seven times?" Jesus replies, "Not seven but seventy-seven times."

We are called on to forgive many among the suffering.

We know those who have stolen to feed their drug or alcohol habit.

We know those who have looked down on persons struggling to make ends meet.

We know those who have treated children harshly.

We know those who have treated older persons with a lack of respect.

We know those who have discouraged loved ones from seeking the treatment they need.

We know those who have told a bereaved person to get over their grief.

We remember those who are sick or bereaved *(time of silent reflection)*.

We are resolved to help bring change. We are resolved to
support the process of change.
Peter asks Jesus, "How often should I forgive, seven times?"
Jesus replies, "Not seven but seventy-seven times."

We are called on to forgive many in the church:
members and friends who do not see the need for the careful
welcoming of newcomers,
members and friends who see young children as a disturbance
rather than a joyful opportunity,
members and friends who see the practical and financial
responsibilities of the church as someone else's task,
members and friends who do not listen to other views on the
pattern or style of worship,
members and friends who support the local church, but not
missions or the wider church.
We are resolved to help bring change. We are resolved to
support the process of change.
Peter asks Jesus, "How often should I forgive, seven times?"
Jesus replies, "Not seven but seventy-seven times."

We need to forgive and be forgiven:
to forgive ourselves for inflicting hurt on another,
to forgive ourselves for not venturing out and taking risks,
to forgive ourselves for avoiding controversy when we were
called to become involved,
to forgive ourselves for not saying the words of thanks or
encouragement,
to forgive others who have gnawed away at our self-confidence,
to forgive others who have poured cold water on our enthusiasm,
to forgive others for ignoring or disparaging our faith.
We will consider fresh insights and be ready for change.
Peter asks Jesus, "How often should I forgive, seven times?"
Jesus replies, "Not seven but seventy-seven times."

Another Way

1. **Sing one verse of a forgiveness hymn between each prayer
section. For example, sing verse one of *Forgive Our Sins as We
Forgive* (*Voices United* #364), or use all verses, one verse after
each section.**

2. Have two persons come to the front of the church and stand
   back to back, arms folded and looking sullen. At the time of the
   "Peter asks Jesus" phrase, both turn to face each other and hug.

3. Use silence in the prayer.

We are called on to forgive many in the church:
members and friends who do not see the need for the careful
welcoming of newcomers,
members and friends who see young children as a disturbance
rather than a joyful opportunity *(time of silent reflection)*.
We think of them.
We forgive them.
Members and friends who see the practical and financial
responsibilities of the church, as someone else's task,
members and friends who do not listen to other views on the
pattern or style of worship,
members and friends who support the local church, but not
missions or the wider church *(time of silent reflection)*.
We think of them.
We forgive them.
We are resolved to help bring change. We are resolved to
support the process of change.
Peter asks Jesus, "How often should I forgive, seven times?"
Jesus replies, "Not seven but seventy-seven times."

Follow the same pattern for the other sections.

Sunday between
September 18 & 24 inclusive
Proper 20 [25]

LECTIONARY READINGS

Exodus 16:2–15   **or**   Jonah 3:10—4:11
Psalm 105:1–6, 37–45   Psalm 145:1–8

Philippians 1:21–30
Matthew 20:1–16

A generous and just response to dayworkers in the vineyard.

**We pray for fair treatment and justice, O God, in our
   troubled world,**
so that the resources of the developed nations are shared;
so that those who pollute pay for the pollution;
so that no child goes hungry, and no woman lives in fear;
so that there is security and a good home for each man and
   woman at the end of the workday;
so that education is offered to each young person, rich or poor;
so that retraining is available to those who are out of a job and
   need to start again.
**Give the peacemakers a chief place among the world's
statespersons, O God,**
so that leaders of countries in conflict listen carefully to each
   other;
so that the voices of the young and the generations yet unborn
   are taken into account;
so that innocent civilians in the crossfire are noticed, and
   child soldiers are freed from their terrible entrapment;
so that journalists covering a conflict are not harmed.
**Inspire us, O God, to be among those who will not rest
until your just and sharing kingdom comes.**

**We pray for fair treatment and justice, O God, among
   those who suffer.**
May health professionals *(like nurse practitioners)* who
   are denied healing opportunities because of professional
   barriers find a listening ear among the legislators.

May those who have no family or friends to care or speak up
for them find supporters and advocates.

May the needs of those denied treatment because of prejudice
or long waiting lists become public, so that administrators
and politicians are compelled to take action.

We pray for those sick at home or in hospital today *(time of
silent reflection)*.

May those who have suffered loss – of a job, a loved one or
friend, or of self-confidence – find those who will listen
deeply to their frustration, their anger, and their emptiness.

We pray for those who have suffered loss *(time of silent reflection)*.

**Inspire us, O God, to be among those who will not rest
until your just and sharing kingdom comes.**

We pray for fair treatment and justice within the church.

Enable us to be open to innovative ways of worship and
serving the neighbourhood.

Enable us to listen to the wisdom of the old, and the simple,
joyful needs of the young and young at heart.

Enable us to think nationally and globally as well as locally
when we give money and receive education.

Enable us to thank openly and generously those who give time
and talent to this faith community, especially those who are
our teachers and leaders.

We name them in silence *(time of silent reflection)*.

**Inspire us, O God, to be among those who will not rest
until your just and sharing kingdom comes.**

And, O God, we pray that we will be just followers of Jesus Christ.

Give us the way of Christ so that we are aware of the
powerless and offer them help.

Give us the way of Christ so that we are slow to judge and
quick to forgive.

Give us the way of Christ so that we confront the self-serving
and refuse to be cowed by the powerful.

Give us the way of Christ so that we take time each day to
meditate and pray.

Give us the way of Christ so that we are aware of the superficial, and ready to laugh at ourselves and our inconsistencies.

**Inspire us, O God, to be among those who will not rest
until your just and sharing kingdom comes.**

Another Way

1. **Explain to the congregation that this is an eyes-open prayer. Have one or more people come to the front of the church carrying different placards for each prayer section. The placards might read, "A good breakfast for every child," "Reduce waiting lists for operations," "Julie for justice." Hold up the placard at the appropriate section.**

2. **Sing a hymn or song of justice (*God, Make Us Servants of Your Peace, Voices United* #676) and put in prayer phrases at the end of each verse.**

God make us servants of your peace,
where there is hate, may we sow love,
where there is hurt, may we forgive,
where there is strife, may we make one.
We pray for the troubled country of *(use current situation)*.
We support the peacemakers there as we are able.
We pray for those who are on strike at *(use current situation)*.
Number us among those who work for peaceful resolution of
   conflict.
We pray for families where members are not getting along.
Give us the courage to hear and stay beside those who are
   hurting.

Follow the same pattern for the other sections.

Sunday between
September 25 & October 1 inclusive
Proper 21 [26]

LECTIONARY READINGS

Exodus 17:1–7 **or** Ezekiel 18:1–4, 25–32
Psalm 78:1–4, 12–16 Psalm 25:1–9

Philippians: 2:1–13
Matthew 21:23–32

Jesus is questioned about the source of his authority.

Who has authority to bring change in our world?
We respect leaders who react promptly to natural and man-
made disasters.
We think of *(use current situation)*.
We respond to politicians/activists who are concerned with
the long-term effects of air, soil, and water pollution. We
think of *(time of silent reflection)*.
We value leaders who are aware of those lacking adequate
housing, nutritious food for their children, and the
opportunity for higher education, and who are prepared to
work for change *(time of silent reflection)*.
We respect leaders the world over who speak out about and
work for gender equality.
The authority of Jesus came from the Living God,
**and God stands ready to empower us to bring change for
good.**

***Who has authority to bring change to those who are going
through tough times?***
We respect employers who are sensitive to the family needs of their
employees and are understanding when personal crises arise.
We value family members and friends who understand when a
cherished one is going through a challenging time and stick
with them.
We respond to medical professionals who take the time to
explain a diagnosis carefully and ask for questions from
their patients.

We value those who recognize the devastating effects of
bereavement or loss, and provide long-term support.
We pray for those we know in our own family and in our
church family *(time of silent reflection)*.
The authority of Jesus came from the Living God,
and God stands ready to empower us to bring change for
good.

Who has authority to bring change in the church?
We respect elders who know and share the history of the faith
community, its celebrations and its trials.
We value members who in spite of work responsibilities (and
a busy family life) are willing to take on vital church work.
We respond to movers and shakers who are ready to take on
opposition to their pursuit of a relevant and faithful church.
We value leaders who are aware of wider church needs and
are prepared to articulate and stand up for them *(time of
silent reflection)*.
The authority of Jesus came from the Living God,
and God stands ready to empower us to bring change for
good.

Who has authority in our own lives?
We respect family members and good friends who listen
deeply to our opinions before venturing their own view.
We are thankful for teachers, youth leaders, and ministers
who have enabled us to form values and goals.
We value the leadership of the saints of our times – Jean Vanier,
Martin Luther King, Mother Teresa – who have words of
compassion, liberation, and caring for each one of us.
We value the leaders of our denomination who speak of
justice and the Christian way *(names)*.
We respond to the word that guides and challenges us day
by day, and we are grateful for those who have shaped us
through our education and life's work.
In silence we name those who are or have been positive
authority figures for us. *(Pause.)*
The authority of Jesus came from the Living God,
and God stands ready to empower us to bring change for
good.

Another Way

1. Before each section, dialogue with the congregation about positive authority figures among world leaders, caregivers, church leaders, and in their personal lives. If possible, include some of the names in the prayer.

2. To remember the leadership of Jesus, sing verse one of *Jesus, Teacher, Brave and Bold* (*Voices United* #605) before the prayer, and verse two after the prayer.

3. Talk briefly about the nature of authority. Sometimes, those who hold power because they have been elected or chosen exercise power and control in a way that seems to contradict the pattern and teachings of the scriptures.

Sunday between
October 2 & 8 inclusive
Proper 22 [27]

LECTIONARY READINGS

Exodus 20:1–4, 7–9, 12–20   **or**   Isaiah 5:1–7
Psalm 19   Psalm 80:7–15

Philippians 3:4b–14
Matthew 21:33–46

*The stone that the builders rejected as worthless
has become the most important.*

God's eyes see differently than the eyes of the world.
The world gives pride of place to politicians, stage and film
    stars, and celebrities.
Heads of government, such as *(give names)* are feted and given
    the best of everything.
(Names of actors) walk the red carpet and are in the spotlight
    at the Oscars.
But God's eyes notice the few protestors carrying placards with
    slogans against global warming, and the students who are
    arrested for standing up against a corrupt regime.
In God's eyes it is the mother with a minimum wage job
    struggling to get by who merits attention, and God's gaze is
    fixed on the agony of the unemployed.
Loving God,
give us your eyes so we may see.

God's eyes see the suffering differently.
We are aware of those who have major illness and take up the
    time of doctors, consultants, and nurses.
We are aware of those who give voice to their emotions over
    the loss of a loved one.
God sees how the infirm older person struggles to make clear
    her concern to a busy health professional.
God sees the child in hospital who is frightened by a strange
    place and unfamiliar people.
God sees and feels the sadness of a child when a cherished pet dies.

God sees and knows the grief felt when a good friend leaves
the neighbourhood for another part of the country.
God sees and feels the desolation of the newly bereaved person.
We remember the sick, the suffering, and those who are
bereaved *(time of silent reflection).*
Loving God,
give us your eyes so we may see.

 God's eyes see the church differently.
We notice the leaders and committee chairs who are
prominent in the life of the faith community.
We notice clergy and lay preachers who lead worship and
preside at Communion.
God sees the woman whose invisible ministry is to bring food
to a shut-in friend,
and the older man who is always available to do odd jobs
around the house for others.
God sees the devotion of a wife to her husband with dementia.
God sees the boy who helps the younger children in the church
school, and the girl who offers to assist her teacher.
Loving God,
give us your eyes so we may see.

 God's eyes see each one of us differently.
Our family and our friends see us as being in control and
confident.
They see us as competent in our job, or settled happily into
retirement.
God sees the struggles that are ours in the testing times of life.
God sees our yearning for a time when life is good and
relationships fulfilling.
God sees our longing for another way of being.
God sees our need to develop our spiritual life, with all the
joys and problems that arise.
We know that your eyes are on us, Loving God.
Help us to see ourselves as you do.

Another Way

1. **Have four blindfolded people sitting on chairs at the front of
the church. As each section of the prayer is completed, have**

one person remove their blindfold, stand up, and express joy. "It's wonderful to see now!"

---

2. **Focus on acceptance and rejection. The parable tells of the son's rejection and death and we see the parallel with Jesus.**

Accepted!
Stars of screen and TV *(names)*, popular sports stars *(names)*.
Rejected!
The homeless, and racial minorities.
Accepted!
Those with money and a fulfilling job.
Rejected!
Those searching unsuccessfully for a job, and the working poor.
With whom do we stand? With whom does God stand?

Accepted!
Those with socially acceptable medical problems: hip replacements, heart disease.
Rejected!
Those with problems not to be mentioned in polite company: sexually transmitted diseases, depression.
Accepted!
Those able to tell their medical professional clearly why they have come to the clinic.
Rejected!
Persons who are not able to articulate their problems.
Accepted!
Those who are able to quickly work through their grief and resume normal activity.
Rejected!
Persons who feel that their loss will never end, and withdraw from their friendship circle.
With whom do we stand? With whom does God stand?

Follow the same pattern for the other sections.

Worldwide Communion

*.The first Sunday in October is usually observed as
World Wide Communion Sunday.*

A prayer with a confessional edge

Bread broken, wine poured out.
Refugees callously exploited, women passed over for advancement.
Bread broken.
Children forced to work, skilled immigrants denied their place
in their profession.
Wine poured out.
Challenged ones passed over for work, elderly persons left
without attention.
Bread broken, wine poured out.
Christ is abused, Christ is sacrificed, and we are called to act!

Bread broken, wine poured out.
Overflowing hospital emergency areas, harassed physicians.
Bread broken.
Symptoms untreated because of the high cost of drugs, hospital
wings closed because money has not yet come through.
Elective surgery delayed because physicians and nurses are
not available.
Wine poured out.
Mentally challenged persons without suitable accommodation,
bereaved family members alone in their loss.
Bread broken, wine poured out.
Christ is abused, Christ is sacrificed, and we are called to act!

Bread broken, wine poured out.
Families at risk in countries where Christianity is a minority
religion.
Bread broken.
Church buildings underused when sharing is possible.
Pastoral charges and denominations going their own way
when program sharing could be a reality.
Wine poured out.
The needs of partner churches overseas downplayed, and local
needs emphasized.

Bread broken, wine poured out.
Christ is abused, Christ is sacrificed, and we are called to act!
Christ is devalued, Christ is misunderstood, and we are called to act!

Bread broken, wine poured out.
Our talents and abilities not reckoned significant, our best efforts not appreciated.
Bread broken.
We have great dreams but we lack the will to bring them to reality.
Wine poured out.
Loved ones taken for granted, friendships superficial.
Christ is not trusted; Christ's spirit is not ours.
In the broken bread, with the poured out wine, we are called to prayer!

Another Way

1. **Insert a time of silence into each section of the prayer.**

Bread broken, wine poured out.
Families at risk in countries where Christianity is a minority religion.
Bread broken.
Church buildings underused when sharing is possible.
Denominations going their own way when program sharing could be a reality.
Wine poured out.
The needs of partner churches overseas downplayed, and local needs emphasized.
We think about these things *(time of silent reflection)*.
Bread broken, wine poured out.
Christ is abused, Christ is sacrificed, and we are called to act!

2. **Sing *Eat This Bread* (*Voices United* #466) between each section.**

3. **Have one person break pieces from a loaf of bread or large bun and another pour wine from a pitcher into a cup or glass at the end of each prayer section.**

Sunday between
October 9 & 15 inclusive
Proper 23 [28]

LECTIONARY READINGS

Exodus 32:1–14	**or**	Isaiah 25:1–9
Psalm 106:1–6, 19–23		Psalm 23

Philippians 4:1–9
Matthew 22:1–14

Take God's invitation to the feast seriously.

 God's Kingdom celebrates
when music, drama, and art are appreciated, and performers and
artists are given the recognition and funding they deserve;
when impoverished peoples receive long-term help and
opportunities for education;
when the winners of the Paralympics are as widely applauded
as the winners of Olympic events;
when aboriginal persons and racial minorities are safe from
prejudice;
when no prisoner is left without someone who they can call
on for help;
when no child is forced to work, and children recruited as sex
slaves or for pornography are freed.
And we will work hard
**to bring the despised, ignored, and rejected to God's
great celebration.**

 God's Kingdom celebrates
when time is forgotten as lovers embrace and children lose
themselves in play;
when civilians in a battle zone are carefully protected and
soldiers suffering from stress are counselled;
when those who have planted gardens enjoy the harvest;
when those who have lost an honoured place in an
organization dear to them are befriended;
when the depressed, the mentally ill, and their families are
taken seriously;

when those who are sick find a friend to talk with;
when the bereaved are given all the time they need to grieve.
As we pray, we remember our families, friends, and those in
our church family *(time of silent reflection).*
God's Kingdom celebrates when those who have had a life's
ambition crushed are comforted.
And we will work hard
**to bring the despised, ignored, and rejected to God's
great celebration.**

God's Kingdom celebrates
when the needs of the young and the infirm are heeded in
worship;
when church members establish a presence in the local
community, and find fresh ways to serve those who struggle
and are afraid;
when the faith community is engaged in education and action
for justice in our world.
And we will work hard,
**to bring the despised, ignored, and rejected to God's
great celebration.**

God's Kingdom celebrates
when each one of us has the courage find the vocation or
occupation that we dream of;
when we are free to laugh at our faults and our failings;
when we are ready to lose face and popularity in order to
stand with a friend;
when we admit to our need for peace, and a renewed life of
prayer and meditation;
when we stand on the side of the hopeless and downhearted.
With joy, we join God's great celebration.

Another Way

1. **Use the chorus of** *I Cannot Come to the Banquet* **before each
section.**

I cannot come to the banquet, I cannot come to the banquet,
don't trouble me now.
I have married a wife; I have bought me a cow.
I have fields and commitments that cost a pretty sum.
Pray, hold me excused, I cannot come.

Medical Mission Sisters 1966

2. **Dramatize each prayer section: *Don't make excuses, come and celebrate!***

Helen: I'm too busy to think about the invitation to help your campaign for the homeless. I have a hair appointment, and then I have to meet a friend for lunch.

Marie: I'm too busy to think about your invitation to help the homeless, but I know it is a great and worthwhile idea. Let's sit down and talk about it over a good lunch.

James: I know we are short of money, and I would like to take on the job of organizing the stewardship campaign for St. Andrew's, but I have personal commitments and there is the golf tournament on the weekend you've got the campaign planned for. Afraid you'll have to count me out.

Rory: I would like to take on the job of organizing the stewardship campaign for St. Andrew's; I know we are short of money. I have a golf tournament that weekend, and there is a family party, but you know, I realize that stewardship is more than money. It's giving time and energy and talent to God's work. So I will forget the golf, and give my apologies to my aunt, and yes, I will do this task. Come round, and we will talk about it over a good dinner.

Follow the same pattern for the other sections.

3. **At the end of each section, have a group of congregants with party hats, favours, and balloons whoop and holler and blow whistles and horns.**

Sunday between
October 16 & 22 inclusive
Proper 24 [29]

LECTIONARY READINGS

Exodus 33:12–23 **or** Isaiah 45:1–7

Psalm 99 Psalm 96:1–9 (10–13)

1 Thessalonians 1:1–10

Matthew 22:15–22

Do you pay taxes to the Emperor or not?

Here is the vision: A world where political leaders look to the needs of this challenged planet and plan to keep it good for the next generation and the ones after that.

Here is the reality: The financial interests of some energy companies come before the need to control carbon emissions.

Here is the vision: No one has to sleep on the streets of our cities; there is room inside for all.

Here is the reality: Street people have no place warm and secure to stay.

Here is the vision: Women have equal rights with men; abuse and job discrimination are at an end.

Here is the reality: In Afghanistan and some countries of the Middle East, women are controlled by fathers and husbands; in the West, the "glass ceiling" prevents women from getting the jobs they deserve.

Your vision is for justice and compassion to prevail.
O God, help us bring it to reality.

Here is the vision: Older persons in care homes are treated with care and respect by adequate staff.

Here is the reality: Staff members are in short supply, and the needs of the residents are not always met.

Here is the vision: Each person receives prompt and appropriate care in hospital.

Here is the reality: Long waits in the emergency department; long waiting lists to see a consultant.

We pray for those who are in seniors homes today and for

those in hospital; those experiencing good care, and those frustrated by their care *(time of silent reflection)*.

Here is the vision: People receive compassionate support when they suffer loss.

Here is the reality: Many are unable to deal with the hard place which is bereavement and find it difficult to get the gentle, long term support they need.

We pray for those who have suffered loss *(time of silent reflection)*.

Your vision is for justice and compassion to prevail.

O God, help us to bring it to reality.

Here is the vision: A church where each newcomer is noticed, welcomed, and made to feel at home.

Here is the reality: Some newcomers are missed and find it difficult to feel a part of the faith community.

Here is the vision: A church where each member feels accepted; their gifts are encouraged, honoured, and used.

Here is the reality: Some people are not part of the "in crowd"; some have not been challenged to use their special gifts.

Here is the vision: A church where the needs of young persons and children are listened to and their questions valued.

Here is the reality: The voices of some young persons are not heard, and their opinions not taken seriously.

You have a vision for your community of faith, O God:

A church where each person, regardless of age or ability, is fully accepted and able to make their presence felt.

Your vision is for justice and compassion to prevail.

O God, help us to bring it to reality.

Here is the vision: Each one of us ready to speak out for the downhearted and afraid.

Here is the reality: we don't quite get round to attending the information meeting or supporting the protest.

Here is the vision: Each one of us confident and ready to venture out.

Here is the reality: A sense of personal doubt, an unwillingness to take necessary risks.

Here is the vision for each one of us: strong bonds of love and friendship linking us with each other.

Here is the reality: a sense of separation; difficulty in keeping friendships vibrant.

You have a vision for each of us, Loving God. Show us that vision and let us embrace your confidence in us.

Another Way

1. Sing the first verse of *Be Thou My Vision* (*Voices United* #642) after each section of the prayer.

2. Have a congregational member talk very briefly about a visionary of our time: a local person who had a vision for the community that has come to pass, or someone like Greg Mortenson (*Three Cups of Tea*) who has brought schools for girls to remote parts of Afghanistan and Pakistan.

3. Silently reflect on your own vision for the world, the church, suffering, or yourself during the prayer.

 Here is the vision: A church where each newcomer is noticed, welcomed, and made to feel at home.
Here is the reality: Some newcomers are missed and find it difficult to feel that they are part of the faith community.
(Reflection around your vision for the church.)
Here is the vision: A church where each member feels that they are accepted and their gifts encouraged, honoured, and used.
Here is the reality: Some people are not part of the "in crowd"; some have not been challenged to use their special gifts.
(Reflection around your vision for the church.)
Here is the vision: A church where the needs of young persons and children are listened to and their questions valued.
Here is the reality: The voices of some young persons are not heard, and their opinions not taken seriously.
You have a vision for your community of faith, O God:
A church where each person, regardless of age or ability, is fully accepted and able to make their presence felt.
(Reflection around your vision of the church.)
Your vision is for justice and compassion to prevail.
O God, help us to bring it to reality.

Follow the same pattern for the other sections.

Sunday between
October 23 & 29 inclusive
Proper 25 [30]

LECTIONARY READINGS

Deuteronomy 34:1–12   Leviticus 19:1–2, 15–18
Psalm 90:1–6, 13–17   **or**   Psalm 1

1 Thessalonians 2:1–8
Matthew 22:34–46

> *Love God with all your heart and soul and mind, and
> your neighbour as you love yourself.*

***Love God and your neighbour as you love yourself. What
does this mean in practice?***

It means taking the time to find out about world issues that
confront us in the newspaper and on TV, about *(recent
headline stories)*.

It means getting involved in the problems of the world, talking
with our elected representatives, writing to the heads of
government overseas.

It means engaging in local issues such as *(name local issues)*
and being a part of the solution.

It means talking to our family and friends about political
topics, and having opinions based on the facts.

**We do love God with heart and soul and mind,
and we are prepared to actively love our neighbour.**

***Love God and your neighbour as you love yourself. What
does this mean in practice?***

Neighbour-loving calls us to express our distaste when the
poor are marginalized and the elderly ignored.

Neighbour-loving calls us to make sure that aboriginal persons
in remote areas have trusted resources for birthing and
educating their children.

Neighbour-loving calls us to address the issue of low-cost
housing in our area.

Neighbour-loving calls us to take time to support the sick and
stand beside those who grieve a loss: of opportunity, of good

health, of one of their senses, or a loved one *(time of silent reflection)*.
We do love God with heart and soul and mind,
and we are prepared to actively love our neighbour.

Love God and your neighbour as you love yourself. What
does this mean in practice?
We respect the gifts and skills of our church neighbours and
encourage their use in faith community.
We respect the practical needs of our church neighbours and
do our best to meet those needs.
We respect the spiritual hunger of our church neighbours
and try our very best to ensure that the hunger is satisfied
through *(Bible study, prayer groups, book study, etc.)*.
We realize that our church neighbours also live overseas, and
through mission funds we help those who have no water, no
education, and no employment.
We do love God with heart and soul and mind,
and we are prepared to actively love our neighbour.

Love God and your neighbour as you love yourself. What
does this mean for each of us?
It means that we reflect carefully about who our neighbour is
at this time and in this place.
It means we turn our concern from the latest trend to the
crying needs around us.
It means we re-evaluate our priorities in the light of Jesus Christ.
It means we have the confidence to bring change in spite of
opposition or hostility.
It means we laugh at our mistakes and pick ourselves up when
we slip on the inevitable banana skin.
We are ready to walk patiently and sensitively in our
neighbour's shoes.

Another Way

1. **Choose four verses of *When I Needed a Neighbour* (*Voices**
United* #600) and sing one after each prayer section.

2. Have the worship leader interview a congregational member about a good neighbour and what this neighbour has done to help others. Have a member talk about someone overseas whom they have helped with money or gifts.

3. Turn a section into a dialogue with the congregation. One section of dialogue will probably be enough.

Love God and your neighbour as you love yourself. What does this mean in practice?
We respect the gifts and skills of our church neighbours and encourage their use in faith community. *How might we do this?*
We respect the practical needs of our church neighbours and do our best to meet those needs. *Can you think of ways we have done this in the past?*
We respect the spiritual hunger of our church neighbours and try our very best to ensure that the hunger is satisfied. *What might we do to satisfy spiritual hunger?*
We realize that our church neighbours also live overseas, and through mission funds we help those who have no water, no education, and no employment. *Are there any mission projects that especially interest you?*
We do love God with heart and soul and mind,
and we are prepared to actively love our neighbour.

Sunday between
October 30 & November 5 inclusive
Proper 26 [31]

LECTIONARY READINGS

Joshua 3:7–17	**or**	Micah 3:5–12
Psalm 107:1–7, 33–37		.Psalm 43

1 Thessalonians 2:9–13
Matthew 23:1–12

> *Jesus calls on the people of his time to watch out for
> those who are proud and to practice humility.*

Friends, practice humility.
Proud business persons drive their own high-powered cars
   and defend their bonuses.
The poor use the bus and count their pennies.
Proud leaders build palaces and put up statues to honour
   themselves.
Good leaders listen to elders and invite children to talk to
   them.
Proud teachers point out only their best students and praise
   their abilities.
Good teachers sit down with their weakest students and offer
   them the help they need.
The great will be humbled,
and the humble made great.

Friends, practice humility.
Will government workers help those with difficult questions
   in a considerate way?
Only if they hear the anxiety of those who seek advice, and
   treat them as they themselves would want to be treated.
Will doctors and health professionals help those who are
   suffering in the most caring way?
Only if they are prepared to hear the patient's story and
   respond with empathy.
Will those who encounter the bereaved and desolate meet
   their deepest needs?

Only if they recognize their loss and respond with comfort and quiet support.
We remember the sick and the bereaved *(time of silent reflection).*
The great will be humbled,
and the humble made great.

 Friends, practice humility.
There are church leaders who draw attention to themselves.
We look for leaders who search out the gifts of fellow members and draw attention to them.
In the church there are those who are concerned only for the local faith community, its buildings and balance sheet.
We look for those who have a wider vision for the church and are ready to risk in faith.
In the church there are those who see the way of Christ as the only true way.
We look for those who see there are many paths to God and who consider the words of the Buddha and the actions of Mahatma Gandhi as well as the teachings of Jesus Christ.
The great will be humbled,
and the humble made great.

 Friends, practice humility.
O Lord it's hard to be humble.
Pride rules us when we are sure our opinion is the only right one.
Can we be open and accepting of the views of others?
Pride rules us when we see our abilities as superior to those of others.
Can we know, appreciate, and use the gifts of our family members, friends, and colleagues?
Pride rules us when we affirm long-established traditions as the only ones to follow.
Can we know, examine, and try out new ways and forge new traditions?
The great will be humbled,
and the humble made great.

Another Way

1. Weave *The Servant Song* (*Voices United* #595) into the prayer, or sing the chorus of *Jesu, Jesu, Fill Us with Your Love* (*Voices United* #593) before each section of the prayer.

2. Allow more time for reflection in the prayer.

Friends, practice humility.
O Lord it's hard to be humble.
Pride rules us when we are sure our opinion is the only right one.
Can we be open and accepting of the views of others? *(Time of silent reflection.)*
Pride rules us when we see our abilities as superior to those of others.
Can we know, appreciate, and use the gifts of our family members, friends, and colleagues? *(Time of silent reflection.)*
Pride rules us when we affirm long-established traditions as the only ones to follow.
Can we know, examine, and try out new ways and forge new traditions? *(Time of silent reflection.)*
The great will be humbled,
and the humble made great.

3. Sing *O Lord it's hard to be humble when you're perfect in every way.*

Sunday between
November 6 & 12 inclusive
Proper 27 [32]

LECTIONARY READINGS

Joshua 24:1–3a, 14–25   **or**   Wisdom of Solomon 6:12–16
Psalm 78:1–7   or Amos 5:18–24
Wisdom of Solomon 6:17–20
or Psalm 70

1 Thessalonians 4:13–18
Matthew 25:1–13

Be ready, you never know the day or the hour.

Be ready to build God's world as God wants it to be:
a world where the computer geeks and experts joyfully help
the struggling and fearful;
a world where the hugely rich give help to the stunningly poor;
a world where urban growth slows to allow space for animals,
birds, and plants;
a local community where authorities provide all-day care for
the elderly infirm and the very young;
a neighbourhood where schoolchildren can find emergency
refuge, and police respond with speed.
With a spirit of urgency,
we will make sure that God's necessary work is done.

Be ready to care with compassion for the troubled and
hard done by,
so that the stress on military personnel is taken seriously, and
the pressures on pilots and air traffic controllers appreciated;
so that the chronically sick are not forgotten, and elective
surgery gets done in reasonable time;
so that fetal alcohol spectrum disorder is recognized, and
youngsters with autism are quickly diagnosed;
so that the bereaved are given time to grieve, and spiritual
caregivers are respected. There are those who come to mind
(time of silent reflection).
With a spirit of urgency,
we will make sure that God's necessary work is done.

Be ready to shape the church as Jesus Christ would want it to be shaped.
We live in an increasingly secular age.
We cannot delay the visioning of new approaches to the scriptures.
We will be aware of contemporary ways of communicating, such as Twitter, Facebook, and PowerPoint, and use them in worship and faith education.
We must urgently work towards the sharing of resources of pastoral charges and denominations.
It is not good enough to say, "We will get round to the needs of the wider church as soon as our local needs are met."
With a spirit of urgency,
we will make sure that God's necessary work is done.

 Be ready for the challenges that come your way.
Be alert for God's call to you even if it is surprising and unexpected.
Prepare for new forms of employment and the challenges of retirement.
Face up to fast-failing relationships and welcome fresh friendship opportunities.
Be ready for the challenging questions of the very young, and the questions of faith that come from those who have no religious belief.
Anticipate the gradual decline of our body and the certainty of death.
With a spirit of urgency,
we will make sure that God's necessary work is done.

Another Way

1. As the prayer is offered, have one person lying on a lawn chair, yawning occasionally, while another scans the horizon with binoculars, ready to act.

2. Sing one verse of *Sleepers, Wake* (based on the scripture passage) (*Voices United* #711) after each of the first three sections, or sing the first part of the first verse (*Sleepers, wake! The watch are calling...bridegroom draweth near!*) after each section.

3. Dialogue with the congregation around the need to be ready, to be on your toes, to anticipate and deal with challenges that arise.

> *What do you see right now as the major threats to world peace, the environment, and to the needs of persons who live in cities or rural areas?*
>
> *Thinking about human suffering, what do you see as the major challenges to those who need hospital treatment, to those who are out of a job, to the bereaved, to children overseas?*

Formulate these into a prayer or invite a congregant do this.

Sunday between
November 13 & 19 inclusive
Proper 28 [33]

LECTIONARY READINGS

Judges 4:1–7   **or**   Zephaniah 1:7, 12–18
Psalm 123   Psalm 90:1–8 (9–11), 12

1 Thessalonians 5:1–11
Matthew 25:14–30

*A parable that encourages you to use the gifts God
has given you to the full.*

**You give us all different gifts, Loving God. Help us to use
them wisely.**

You give us the gift of care, to ensure our waste disposal is
carefully done.

You give us the gift of music, to explore, take pleasure from,
and offer praise to you. You give us the gifts of relaxation
and sleep to enjoy and dream and daydream in.

You give us the gifts of writing and speaking out, so that
political prisoners are not forgotten.

You give us the gift of encouragement, to ensure that we all
use our gifts.

You give us the gift of patience. We do not expect our world to
change overnight, but we hang in and keep plugging away.

You give us the gift of support for others so that we notice and
help as we are able.

We will not give in. We will not give up.
We will keep on using our gifts.

**You give us all different gifts, Loving God. Help us to use
them wisely.**

You give us creativity and the joy of using piano, paintbrush,
humour, and drama to bring pleasure to others.

You give us the gifts of compassion and good humour, and
the opportunity to use them among the troubled, the
downhearted, the sick, and the fragile.

You give us the gift of persistence, and the willingness to
persist with those who cannot.

You give us the gift of consolation, and opportunities to use it
when tears and dark hopelessness are the signs of loss.

We bring to you those who are on our mind today *(time of
silent reflection)*.

We will not give in. We will not give up.
We will keep on using our gifts.

 *You give us all different gifts, Loving God. Help us to use
them wisely.*

You give us the ability to praise and pray; we celebrate our
presence in worship.

You give us silence in our souls and the chance to listen for
your holy voice.

You give us the friendship of fellow Christians and all the
eating, listening, reading, and learning we do together.

You give us faith and your love that make a mockery of time
limits and barriers – any time limits, any barriers.

We will not give in. We will not give up.
We will keep on using our gifts.

 *You give us all different gifts, Loving God. Help us to use
them wisely.*

As your gifted people we pledge:

to acknowledge gifts that others see in us and try them out;

to speak out about the gifts we see in others and encourage
their use;

to express thanks when we have received a gift, an
opportunity, or a kindly gesture;

to search out the gifts that are needed to relieve our stressed
planet and use them;

to be counted among those who strive for justice and equality
in our communities today, and to persist in the face of
opposition and antagonism.

We will not give in. We will not give up.
We will keep on using our gifts.

Another Way

1. Sing the chorus of *Go, Make a Diff'rence* (*More Voices* #209) after each section of the prayer.

2. Individual congregational members might take turns reading phrases of the prayer, or some gifts might be mimed.

3. Turn the "you" and "we" statements to "I" statements and have a different person offer each section of the prayer.

 You give us all different gifts, Loving God. Help us to use them wisely.
You give us creativity and so I am able to play the piano and through my acting bring pleasure to others.
You give us the gift of compassion and so I have the opportunity to give encouragement to my friends and visit people who are ill.
You give us the gift of persistence, and I will not give up on *(local cause)* even though it is sometimes frustrating to be a part of it.
You give us the gift of consolation, and I am glad to comfort my friends when they suffer loss.
I bring to you those who are on my mind today *(time of silent reflection)*.
I will not give in. I will not give up.
I will keep on using my gifts.

Thanksgiving Day
Second Monday in October (Canada)/
Fourth Thursday in November (USA)

LECTIONARY READINGS
Deuteronomy 8:7–18
Psalm 65
2 Corinthians 9:6–15
Luke 17:11–19

The person who came back to say thank you!

A prayer for Thanksgiving Sunday

Thanksgiving Celebrations!
The harvest safely gathered in from field, orchard, vineyard,
   and garden;
the barns, storage places, and freezers full to overflowing.
A fair reward given and received for much hard work.
We give thanks for those who put food on our table, *(pause for
   silent reflection)* and we pray:
for those who are struggling to make ends meet as farmers,
   fishers, or orchardists;
for those who are homeless or have lost loved ones and
   livestock as a result of floods and other natural disasters;
for world leaders who strive to encourage those who have
   plenty to share with those who go hungry;
for hungry refugees waiting for a country to accept them.
We ask a simple question.
Creator God,
What can we do to help?

Thanksgiving celebrations!
A new job found, our own or another's health restored, the
   ache of bereavement eased.
We give thanks for those we know, for members of our church
   family *(pause for silent reflection)*, and we pray for:
those who cannot harvest their crops or tend their livestock
   because of injury;
those who are newly out of a job and are searching for
   employment;

those who ache to gather in the harvest but are too old or
infirm;

those for whom there is no end is in sight for their illness or
their grief *(time of silent reflection)*.

We ask a simple question.

Creator God,
What can we do to help?

Thanksgiving celebrations!

We give thanks for our work together as a faith community
this fall, for every sign of co-operation among churches in
our town/city, and for all who support the mission work of
our church.

We give thanks, and we pray:

for those in our church who face challenging times;

for those who promote sharing among pastoral charges of our
denomination;

for those who work tirelessly for co-operation among local
faith groups.

We ask a simple question.

Creator God,
What can we do to help?

Thanksgiving celebrations!

Our family and friends joyfully gathering around the festive
table, remembering good times, sharing family news, the air
full of laughter and talk of what the future holds *(pause for
silent reflection)*.

We give thanks, and we pray:

for family members and friends who are facing tough
challenges;

for those who cannot forgive angry words and harsh acts –
their own or of others;

for those separated by distance or conflict;

for those who have no Thanksgiving table at which they are
welcome.

We ask a simple question.

Creator God,
What can we do to help?

Another Way

1. Have congregation members share with those around them what they are thankful for.

2. Sing the first verse of *Come, You Thankful People, Come* (*Voices United* #516) or the chorus of *We Give Our Thanks* (*More Voices* #187) after each prayer section.

3. After each prayer section, have a congregant put a gift on the Communion table and state why she/he has placed the gift.

I give this gift of food with thanks to God for all I have received; I want it to be used in the local food bank.

I give this gift of money with thanks to God for all I have received; I want it to be used for the mission work of the church.

All Saints Sunday
November 1 or the first Sunday in November

LECTIONARY READINGS
Revelation 7:9–17
Psalm 34:1–10, 22
1 John 3:1–3
Matthew 5:1–12

The Sermon on the Mount.

It is not the powerful, the rich, and the famous who are the top people in God's Kingdom,
but those who know their spiritual poverty, those who mourn, the pure in heart, and the peacemakers…God's saints.

The saints have gone before us as examples of justice-bringers.
Oscar Romero reminds us of the need to stand with the poor and powerless.
Martin Luther King Junior reminds us that racial prejudice is not acceptable.
Dietrich Bonhoeffer reminds us that the evil ones have to be faced.
(Name a local or church person who is considered a saint and what they remind us to do.)
Give us the strength, O God, moral and spiritual, to be counted as followers of Jesus, the man of justice.
We strive for Christ's compassion.
We strive to be counted among the saints.

The saints have gone before us as examples of those who show compassion.
Mother Julian calls us to listen carefully to those who are deeply troubled.
Francis of Assisi calls us to support and give practical help to those who are sick.
We pray for those whose names we know, and those who are on our minds this morning *(time of silent reflection)*.
Mother Teresa calls us to stand beside the dying, those who have lost loved ones, and those who have suffered other losses.

Give us the will, O God, the individual and the community
will, to be counted as followers of Jesus who heal the sick,
and whose care for the bereaved is heartfelt.
We strive for Christ's compassion.
We strive to be counted among the saints.

 *The saints have gone before us as those who founded and
encouraged the church.*
Paul the apostle shows us the tenacity of one who tended and
supported fragile faith communities.
Patrick of Ireland shows us how missionary zeal wins
converts and defeats the powers of darkness.
Jean Vanier of Canada shows us how to live in loving
community and make community living fun.
Jesus loved his disciple family. Give us the desire, O God, to
work with others in faith community, as followers of Jesus.
We strive for Christ's compassion.
We strive to be counted among the saints.

 We are challenged to sainthood in our day and generation:
to counter the influence of selfishness, but stay involved in the
rough and tumble of daily life;
to name the forces of darkness, but not be blinded by self-serving;
to serve the oppressed humbly, but not neglect our own family
and friends;
to nurture our own life of faith, but not be so pious and
heavenly that we are no earthly use.
Give us the certainty, O God, that work in the name and spirit
of Jesus Christ is fulfilling and life-bringing.
We strive for Christ's compassion.
We strive to be counted among the saints.

Another Way

1. Sing:

Oh, when the saints go marching in
Oh, when the saints go marching in
Lord, how I want to be in that number
When the saints go marching in

after each section and several times at the end of the prayer.

2. During the prayer, role play an interview with one or two famous saints about why they kept with their cause in spite of threats and danger. For example, interview Martin Luther King on the freedom movement, or Mother Teresa on caring for the dying in Calcutta. The interviews can be very short. There is much information on the World Wide Web!

3. While the prayer is being offered, pictures of saints might be passed around the congregation or projected onto a screen. Make sure you include some local or faith community "saints."

Reign of Christ Sunday
Between November 20 & 26 inclusive
Proper 29 [34]

LECTIONARY READINGS

Ezekiel 34:11–16, 20–24   **or**   Ezekiel 34:11–16, 20–24
Psalm 100   Psalm 95:1–7a

Ephesians 1:15–23
Matthew 25:31–46

*The King, whose rule includes welcoming the stranger,
caring for the sick, feeding the hungry, and visiting
the prisoner – a different type of kingdom.*

Come Christ and reign among us!
In the midst of warring groups in *(current examples)* bring
    listening, bring reconciliation, bring peace.
In the midst of famine *(current examples)* where some persons
    live from day to day not knowing where the next meal is
    coming from, bring food and fair employment.
In the midst of drought, and where water is a scarce
    commodity and women walk miles to the nearest river or
    spring, be with those who enable wells to be drilled.
O risen and just Christ,
we loyally support your rule.

Come Christ and rule among us!
In the midst of those who cannot afford basic clothing, encour-
    age the volunteers who run clothing depots and thrift stores.
Be with those who visit prisoners, and support those who
    speak out against punishment and for prisoner education
    and job training.
In the midst of serious physical and mental illness, bring
    endurance, voices that are ready to speak out, and hope.
In the midst of bereavement and the despair arising from
    personal loss, give deep listening, and a fresh start.
We pray for those in our church family, for those in our own
    families, and for our friends *(time of silent reflection)*.
O risen and just Christ,
we loyally support your rule.

Come Christ and rule among us!

In the midst of our search for a mission with other faith
communities,

bring flexibility, bring sustained enthusiasm, bring a sense of
our common roots.

In the midst of a generation where Christian ways and
worship seem irrelevant,

bring a willingness to warmly welcome the stranger, to offer
joyful praise to God, and to accept the need to study and
learn new things.

And when we find it difficult to use our talents confidently,
dedicate our time ungrudgingly, or face evil directly, give us
a vision of faithful discipleship.

O risen and just Christ,
we loyally support your rule.

Come Christ and rule among us!

When we would put off or delay the act of kindness, give us
the willingness to begin.

When we feel the need to conform to the standards of our age,
show us compassionate gospel alternatives.

When we hang back from speaking out against the unfeeling
power people, give us courage and persistence.

In the midst of our uncertainty and inaction, give us your just
pattern and a willingness to stand beside the downtrodden.

O risen and just Christ,
we loyally support your rule.

Another Way

1. Instead of the leader phrase and response at the end of each
   section, sing the first two lines of *Rejoice, the Lord Is King*
   (*Voices United* #213) or *The Kingdom of God* (*More Voices* #146).

2. Have a dialogue between two persons about the significance
   of the rule of Christ for today.

Lily: I'm not at all sure that the rule of Jesus means anything
today. I mean, he had a ministry 2000 years ago. Isn't his
way of life completely out of date?

Jason: Take a look at the gospel passage for today. Jesus is talking about those we should stand beside: the hungry, the poor, prisoners, those who lack the bare necessities of life. We have people today who need food banks – there is one in our town. There are those in Africa who go to bed hungry. And Big Brothers and Big Sisters are looking for mentors for boys and girls. Think about them for a moment. *(Time of silent reflection.)*

After the time of reflection, you could dialogue with the congregation about who they see as coming within the gospel categories today.

Lily: Okay, okay, you have a point. But all that stuff about miracle healings and demons being exorcised – how can we believe in that fantastic nonsense?

Jason: Well, you have the option of going for a literal view of scripture that takes miracles at face value, or seeing the value system that Jesus made clear in his rule. Going back to today's gospel reading, I see compassion. I will say that again – compassion. Jesus was a marked man because he stood beside those who were needy in his day and age that no one cared about: sex trade workers, shady tax collectors, and the mentally sick. And how he healed is not as important as how he cared. Don't we have persons who need that Jesus-type compassion today?

Think about it. *(Time of silent reflection.)*

After the time of reflection you could dialogue with the congregation about who they see as coming within the gospel categories today.

Follow the same pattern for the other sections.

Memorial/Remembrance/ Veterans' Sunday

Remembering is our responsibility, O God.
We remember those who have died for the cause of freedom.
We remember those who have served, and who today serve in
   (insert place).
We remember those who create peace in our world.
We support the peacemakers. We work to counter the powers
   of fear and darkness.
(Time of silent reflection.)
Our remembering is valuable.
Learning from the past can lead us to right action.

Remembering is our responsibility, O God.
We remember women and men of the armed forces who suffer
   trauma and disabilities from war.
We remember the families of military personnel who wait, and
   who deal with the effects of war on their loved ones.
We remember civilians who suffer and die in the midst of
   conflict.
We remember those for whom illness drags on. There are sick
   persons on our minds and in our hearts this morning. We
   remember them *(time of silent reflection)*.
We remember those who can no longer remember because of
   memory loss.
We remember those who have lost loved ones, for whom the
   pain of loss will not go away *(time of silent reflection)*.
We support healers and pastoral care-givers; we work to
   ensure that the health budget is an adequate one.
Our remembering is valuable.
Learning from the past can lead us to right action.

Remembering is our responsibility, O God.
We remember those in our church who are going through
   hard times.
We remember families in our faith community where
   relationships are strained.
We remember those in homes for the aged and in mental
   institutions *(time of silent reflection)*.

We remember the unknown thousands all over the world
whose lives have been changed by the mission fund *(time of
silent reflection)*.

We support our local faith community and the wider work of
our denomination. We remember the leaders of our wider
church, the work of *(insert specific names)* and the leaders of
our national church *(time of silent reflection)*.

Our remembering is valuable.
Learning from the past can lead us to right action.

 Remembering is our responsibility, O God.

We remember strained and tense relationships in our family
circle.

We remember the skills and talents that we have not explored
nor confronted.

We remember the fear and lack of self-confidence that holds
us back.

We will trust our own abilities.

We thankfully remember those who are our strength and our
security.

We gratefully remember those who challenge us to fresh fields
of endeavour.

We bring to mind those who encourage us to test our faith.

We express our gratitude to those who stand beside us; we
trust our friends.

Our remembering is valuable.
Learning from the past can lead us to right action.

Another Way

1. Have four candles on the Communion table. As each section is
completed, light a candle and place a poppy at its base.

2. Give times of silence in each section of the prayer. You may
wish to reduce the number of phrases in each section.

 Remembering is our responsibility, O God.

We remember strained and tense relationships in our family
circle.

We remember *(time of silent reflection)*.

We thankfully remember those who are our strength and our
security.

We express our gratitude to those who stand beside us; we
trust our friends.

We remember *(time of silent reflection).*

Our remembering is valuable.

Learning from the past can lead us to right action.

3. The first and second sections may be offered by a former
   military person.

A Baptismal Prayer

In you, O God, all the families of the world are blessed.
The family of *(name)* baptized today gives thanks for the joy
    and wonder they have experienced through the birth *(and
    upbringing)* of this so-well-loved child.
This family will find fulfillment as they nurture and
    experience family life with ... *her/him.*
We ask your blessing, O God, so that families in the midst of
    conflict and civil strife, such as in *(insert current event)* will
    find peace;
so that families where the breadwinner is facing job loss and
    financial hardship will find hope for better times ahead;
so that those who know strife in the family circle will discover
    the way to reconciliation,
and work to make it happen.
And we will help
to make your blessing come alive!

In you, O God, the suffering ones are blessed.
We pray that children will be given priority when resources
    are in short supply.
We pray that all who struggle with physical illness will see
    their struggle resolved.
We pray that all who are oppressed with the darkness of
    mental illness will see a glimmer of light.
We pray that all who feel the loss of a loved one will balance
    the emptiness of bereavement with the joy of remembering
    a life well lived.
We remember those we know now suffering *(time of silent
    reflection).*
And we will help
to make your blessing come alive!

In you, O God, the Church is blessed.
With your blessing, this child will find a church that supports,
    teaches and encourages him/her to explore and venture
    with the faith community. With your blessing, members
    and friends of the local faith community will care for and
    challenge each other.

With your blessing, the needs of the neighbourhood will be
understood and find a ready response.
With your blessing, the wider church will know its friends
through gifts from the mission fund.
Our common participation in the life of the church embodies
your blessing!
And we will help
to make your blessing come alive!

 In you, O God, each one of us is blessed.
We realize how many and how varied your gracious gifts to
us are.
We know the possibility of giving and receiving forgiveness.
We recognize our ability to offer and grow in friendship.
We are prepared to confront the powerful ones and work for
your justice and sharing.
O God, how richly, how abundantly, how lovingly you have
blessed us!
O God, how richly, how abundantly, how lovingly you will
bless us!
And we will help
to make your blessing come alive!

Children's Sunday

Children of the world, speak to us!
Call on us to stop the senseless killing of young persons in
    (name place).
Remind us of the troubled faces of refugee boys and girls in
    (Darfur/other refugee camps).
Encourage us to support the children in our city and
    worldwide who are abused, or live on the streets or in sub-
    standard housing. Keep us aware of the needs of local young
    people, like those who *(use the breakfast program, use the
    church premises for a club, enjoy soccer games)*.
The children lead.
Give us the faith to follow.

Suffering children, speak to us!
Take us to the acute care wards and show us the children who
    are sick and perhaps far from home.
Remind us of the adults who stay with the children, enduring
    hardship and loneliness as they do so.
Enable us to share the heartache and emptiness of the families
    whose daughters and sons have died.
And we widen our prayers to include adults who are facing
    serious illness, or an end to active life, and those who are
    bereaved *(time of silent reflection)*.
Encourage us to support children who are sick, and their families.
The children lead.
Give us the faith to follow.

Children of the church, speak to us!
Remind us of those members of this congregation who lead
    and direct our children's groups: Beavers and Cubs, church
    school and nursery *(insert your own groups)*.
Show us the happy faces of children and their parents who are
    supported by the mission fund.
Take us out into the community and point out the unfilled
    needs of local youngsters.
Encourage us to stand beside children and leaders of children
    in their vital tasks.
The children lead.
Give us the faith to follow.

Children and grandchildren, speak to us!
Remind us of the ongoing needs of children and grandchildren
  at various stages of life.
Enable us to listen deeply to the spoken and unspoken needs.
Fill us with thanksgiving for all that our parents, children,
  grandchildren, nephews, and nieces have given us.
Remind us of those who are pregnant and so happy about it,
  and those who are pregnant and worried.
Gracefully be with those who would like to have children and
  cannot conceive.
Encourage us to challenge and support family members who
  mean so much to us, especially those who are suffering or
  bereaved *(time of silent reflection)*.
The children lead.
Give us the faith to follow.

And we ask, O God, that you bless the child within each of us:
the part of us that responds with awe to a beautiful sunset;
the part of us that revels in chasing balloons and wearing
  funny hats at a party;
the part of us that trusts first;
the part of us that is always asking the simple questions;
the part of us that responds from the heart first;
the part of us that cannot resist playing games and telling
  corny jokes.
**Loving and playful God, encourage us to explore and
  develop the child within,
and to give our child within the freedom she/he deserves.**

Another Way

1. **This prayer might be offered by four children or youth.**

2. **Have children speak the prayer directly using the "I" voice.**

Listen to what I have to say.
The war in Afghanistan seems to go on and on. Can't any of those
  smart world leaders do anything to stop it? I am frustrated that
  refugees don't have enough to eat in Darfur, Sudan, and other
  countries. Can't you adults do something about it?

I know that there are children who come to my school without
   breakfast, and some who live in damp and cold houses and
   apartments. Is this right?

And I have a friend who finds it very difficult to read. Why
   can't she get the help she needs at school?

I want you to think about these things. *(Time of silent reflection.)*

If we children lead you, will you follow?
With faith, we will follow.

I feel good about the leaders of our church school here,
   (names) are always ready with some new story or craft idea.
   It's a fun time.

And my friend Simone comes to the church here on a
   Thursday evening for Scouts and enjoys that too.

Ms. Rose told us two weeks ago about a young woman who
   was supported by our mission fund in Kenya. She was given
   some job training and is now able to support herself and
   help her family. That makes me feel very good.

And Ann Maric, our minister, was up at city hall last month
   speaking up for more help for the Boys and Girls club in our
   area. That makes me proud to be part of this church.

I want you to think about these things. *(Time of silent
   reflection.)*

If we children lead you, will you follow?
With faith, we will follow.

**Clearly this form of prayer will have to be tailored to the local
situation. You could also turn it into a dialogue between the child
and the worship leader.**

THEMATIC INDEX

Please note that the page numbers refer to the first page of the Sunday in which that theme is represented.

HEBREW SCRIPTURE INDEX

NEW TESTAMENT SCRIPTURE INDEX

MORE VOICES COLLECTION

Experience the community of song that unites, empowers, and inspires, like nothing else.

More Voices
288 PP | 6" x 9" | PAPER COIL BOUND
ISBN 978-1-55134-148-4

More Voices, a 288-page songbook with 225 songs suited for today's contemporary worship, has something for everyone!

- Powerful Canadian hymns
- African calls to worship
- French contemplative chants
- Foot-stomping praise

The songs are grouped in liturgical order making worship planning easy. Includes user-friendly scriptural, first-line, and topical indexes.

What an excellent opportunity to learn how folks around the world sing their songs of the Spirit! Thanks for this wonderful gift.

– Fran Barton, Music Director, Winfield United Church, Lake Country, BC

More Voices is a wonderful resource that will enrich the musical life of the United Church. Its pages are full of singable music that appeals to all ages!

– Catherine Barkhouse, United Church student minister studying at the Atlantic School of Theology, Halifax, NS

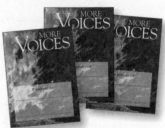

More Voices Large Print

This words-only volume contains the lyrics for every song in the More Voices collection – including all foreign-language lyrics – in a font-size recommended by the CNIB for use by people with visual impairments.

208 PP | 6.5" x 9.5" | PAPER COIL BOUND
ISBN 978-1-55134-182-8

More Voices Accompanist Edition

This new edition in an 8.5" x 11" format with heavier paper is ideal for organists and other musicians.

288 PP | 8.5" x 11" | PAPER COIL BOUND
ISBN 978-1-55134-172-9

More Voices Audio CD

The complete collection of songs sung live – includes every verse of every song!

MP3 FORMAT ON 2 CDs
ISBN 978-1-55145-523-5

More Voices Bookplates

PACKAGES OF 25 ONLY
BLANK CH10489
IN HONOUR OF CH10321
IN MEMORIAM OF CH10320
PRESENTED TO CH10322

More Voices Vinyl Cover

This clear plastic protective jacket reduces the wear that occurs with regular pew use and extends the use of the More Voices Songbook.
ISBN MVCOVER

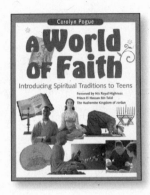

A World of Faith
Introducing Spiritual Traditions to Teens
Carolyn Pogue

This comprehensive book covers most of the world's main religions in a captivating and accessible way. Pogue describes the unique practices of the various faith traditions, institutional rites and beliefs, and touches on the deeper truths common to humanity. Young people tell about their practices and how these influence their lives and world views. Full-colour photographs and comments allow teens to appreciate how different faith traditions affect other lives in a relevant way.

192 PP | 7.25" x 9" | Paper
ISBN 978-1-55145-554-9

Youth Spirit
Program Ideas for Church Groups
Compiled by Cheryl Perry

Organized according to the seasons of the Christian year, this book offers a multitude of flexible ideas to create unique programs for youth aged 12–18. Includes games, learning exercises, integration activities, reflection questions, worship suggestions, and explanations of the church seasons.

192 PP | 8.5" x 11" | Paper
ISBN 978-1-55145-247-0

Youth Spirit 2
More Program Ideas for Youth Groups
Cheryl Perry
128 PP | 8.5" x 11" | Paper
ISBN 978-1-55145-500-6

For more resources for youth, go to www.woodlakebooks.com.

BESTSELLING CHILDREN'S BIBLE STORIES

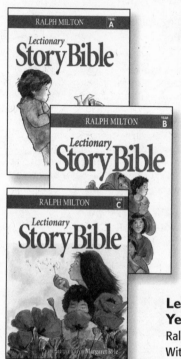

> " Ralph Milton has combined biblical story, historical research, thoughtful theology, and powerful imagination to bring our sacred stories alive. They take my breath away. Margaret Kyle's artwork is stunning, opening the stories in fresh ways, deep in emotion – enchanting.
>
> – Susan Burt, Coordinating Editor of *Seasons of the Spirit*, www.seasonsonline.ca

Lectionary Story Bible – Years A, B, C
Ralph Milton
With the art of Margaret Kyle

The *Lectionary Story Bible Set*, Years A, B, and C, by Ralph Milton, covering all three years of the *Revised Common Lectionary*, is the largest collection of children's Bible stories ever published. Finally, one comprehensive package that is easy to use, easy to understand, and contains all of the familiar and favourite Bible stories. Educators can feel good about sharing these well-crafted, non-violent, life-affirming stories with children and their congregations!

Each book: 240–256 PP | 6.75" x 9.75" | HC
Lectionary Story Bible Set of 3 – Years A, B, and C
ISBN **978-1-55145-577-8 Includes full 3-year index (in Year C)**

Also sold separately:
Lectionary Story Bible – Year A ISBN 978-1-55145-547-1
Lectionary Story Bible – Year B ISBN 978-1-55145-564-8
Lectionary Story Bible – Year C ISBN 978-1-55145-576-1
Includes full 3-year index

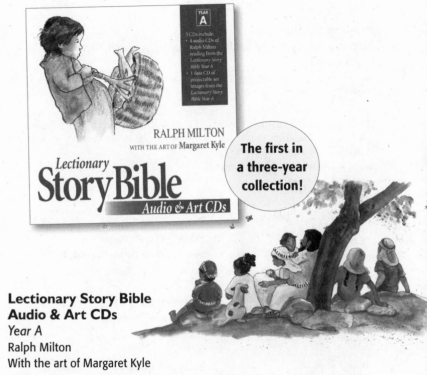